Gītā-Māhātmya

&

Śrīmad-Bhāgavat Māhātmya

Publications by Touchstone Media

Gītā Mahātmya and Śrīmad Bhāgavatam Mahātmya
Prārthanā
Śrī Bhaktivinoda Vāṇī Vaibhava Volume 1, Sambandha
Śrī Bhaktivinoda Vāṇī Vaibhava Volume II, Abhideya and Prayojana
Śrī Prema Bhakti-candika
Sārvabhauma Śataka
Hari Bhakti Kalpa Latika
Śrī Nityānanda-caritāmṛta
Pada Sevana
Sweet Pastimes of Damodara
Dog and the Wolf
Epic Characters of Mahabharat Series
Krishna Pocket Guide
Sri Prema Vilasa
Uddhava Gita

If you are interested in the purchasing or the distribution of this book or any of the above publications, you may contact the publisher at:

Touchstone Media
Block FE 2/3, Sector 3
Salt Lake, Kolkata 700106, India
Tel: 91(33)64513825
e-mail : isvara99@gmail.com

Touch stone media

www.touchstonemedia.com

śrī guru-gaurāṅgau jayataḥ

GĪTĀ-MĀHĀTMYA

of

Padma Purāṇa

LORD ŚIVA'S GLORIFICATION OF THE BHAGAVAD-GĪTĀ

&

ŚRĪMAD-BHĀGAVAT MĀHĀTMYA

of

Skanda Purāṇa

by

Krishna-Dvaipayāna Vyāsa

Touch stone media

śrī kṛṣṇāpaṇam astu
May this be an offering unto Lord Krishna

Compiled and Published by Īśvara dasa
Gītā-Māhātmya translation from Hindi by Sandhya dasi and Anurādhā dāsī
Śrīmad-Bhāgavat Māhāmtya translated by Bhumipati dāsa and edited by Pundarika Vidyanidhi dāsa
Chief Editor and Proofreader : Isodhyana dāsī
Cover Painting by Dhṛtī devi dāsī
Design and Layout by Īśvara dāsa

Sixth Printing - 2011, 2000 copies

ISBN 81- 87897 - 05 - 8

Revised Third Edition

Printed in India

Printed at : CDC Printers (P) Ltd., Kolkata, India

Contents

GĪTĀ-MĀHĀTMYA

Preface 9
Introduction 11
The Glories of Chapter One 14
The Glories of Chapter Two 18
The Glories of Chapter Three 22
The Glories of Chapter Four 25
The Glories of Chapter Five 28
The Glories of Chapter Six 30
The Glories of Chapter Seven 33
The Glories of Chapter Eight 35
The Glories of Chapter Nine 37
The Glories of Chapter Ten 39
The Glories of Chapter Eleven 42
The Glories of Chapter Twelve 46
The Glories of Chapter Thirteen 49
The Glories of Chapter Fourteen 52
The Glories of Chapter Fifteen 54
The Glories of Chapter Sixteen 56
The Glories of Chapter Seventeen 58
The Glories of Chapter Eighteen 60
Index of Slokas& Their Speakers 63
Gītā Māhātmyam by Śrī Śankarācarya 64

ŚRĪMAD-BHĀGAVAT MĀHĀTMYA

Introduction 69
Chapter One
Śāṇḍilya Muni Describes Vrajabhūmi 75
Chapter Two
Parīkṣit and Kṛṣṇa's wives, while chanting the glories of the Lord, met Uddhava 80

Chapter Three
The glories of Śrīmad-Bhāgavatam, the speaker and the hearer's attainment of the supreme abode **84**
Chapter Four
The characteristics of Śrīmad-Bhāgavatam, the symptoms of the speaker and the listener, and establishing the procedure for hearing **91**
Chapter Five
Description of the results of hearing Śrīmad-Bhāgavatam, and the condition of those who are averse to such hearing **96**

GĪTĀ-MĀHĀTMYA

of

Padma Purāṇa

LORD ŚIVA'S GLORIFICATION OF THE BHAGAVAD-GĪTĀ

"Anyone who hears or studies this *Gita Mahatmya* very quickly destroys all sins, which he has accumulated. And that person, who remembers this discourse with great faith attains the results of all kinds of pious activities and great sacrifices, and after enjoying all worldly opulences, attains the abode of Lord Vishnu"

Preface

In the *Mahabharata* (*Shanti Parva* 348.51-52) we can trace out the history of the *Gita* as follows: "In the beginning of the millenium known as Treta-yuga this science of the relationship with the Supreme was delivered by Vivasvan to Manu. Manu, being the father of mankind, gave it to his son Maharaja Iksvaku, the king of this earth planet and forefather of the Raghu dynasty, in which Lord Ramacandra appeared." Therefore, *Bhagavad-gita* existed in human society from the time of Maharaja Iksvaku. At the present moment we have just passed through five thousand years of the Kali-yuga, which lasts 432,000 years. Before this there was Dvapara-yuga (800,000 years), and before that there was Treta-yuga (1,200,000 years). Thus, some 2,005,000 years ago, Manu spoke the *Bhagavad-gita* to his disciple and son Maharaja Iksvaku, the king of this planet earth. The age of the current Manu is calculated to last some 305,300,000 years, of which 120,400,000 have passed. Accepting that before the birth of Manu the *Gita* was spoken by the Lord to His disciple the sun-god Vivasvan, a rough estimate is that the *Gita* was spoken at least 120,400,000 years ago; and in human society it has been existent for two million years. It was spoken by the Lord again to Arjuna about five thousand years ago. That is the rough estimate of the history of the *Gita*, according to the *Gita* itself and according to the version of the speaker, Lord Sri Krishna. It was spoken to the sun-god Vivasvan because he is a ksatriya and is the father of all ksatriyas who are descendants of the sun-god, or the *surya-vamsa ksatriyas*. Because *Bhagavad-gita* is as good as the *Vedas*, being spoken by the Supreme Personality of Godhead, this knowledge is *apauruseya*, superhuman. Since the Vedic instructions are accepted as they are, without human interpretation, the *Gita* must therefore be accepted without mundane interpretation. The mundane wranglers may speculate on the *Gita* in their own ways, but that is not *Bhagavad-gita* as it is. Therefore, *Bhagavad-gita* has to be accepted as it is, from the disciplic succession, and it is described herein that the Lord spoke to the sun-god, the sun-god spoke to his son Manu, and Manu spoke to his son Iksvaku.

From *Bhagavad-gita As It Is*
by His Divine Grace A. C. Bhaktivedanta Swami
Prabhupāda

INTRODUCTION

In the *Hari-vaṁsa* it is stated:

vede rāmāyaṇe caiva purāṇe bhārate tathā
ādāvante ca madhye ca hariḥ sarvatraḥ gīyate

"In all the *Vedas, Ramayana, Puranas,* and *Mahabharata*, Lord Hari's glories are sung throughout in the beginning, the middle, and the end."

Bhagavad-gita is one of the sections of *Mahabharata*, *Bhisma Parva,* and thus it is scripture. Scriptures are narrations about the Supreme Lord or are words spoken by the Supreme Lord. The *Srimad-Bhagavatam* is a beautiful narration of the pastimes of the Supreme Lord and *Bhagavad-gita* is the song of the Supreme Lord Krishna. Both are nondifferent from Him.

There is a story of a *brāhmaṇa* who regularly studied *Bhagavad-gītā*. He was poor and he lived with his wife in a small cottage. After daily studying *Bhagavad-gita,* he would go to beg and in this way maintain himself and his wife. One day as he read *Bhagavad-gita* he came across a verse in the ninth chapter where Lord Krishna says, *yoga-ksemam vahamy aham*—"I will personally carry and deliver the needs of My devotees." When he read this verse he became puzzled and doubtful and thought, "How is it that Bhagavan personally carries and delivers the needs of His devotees? He may inspire someone to carry out the needs of the devotees, such as giving charity. But that Bhagavan personally delivers the needs seems impossible."

Reading the verse again and again, the *brāhmaṇa* could not believe it. He crossed it out with a red pen thinking it a mistake. Afterwards he went to do his daily begging.

That day everyone offered him excuses rather than charity. Some said there was a death in the family, others that their children were sick, and thus they could not give alms that particular day.

Meanwhile, back at the *brāhmaṇa's* house, a young boy arrived and knocked on the door. The *brāhmaṇa's* wife answered and was surprised to find the boy carrying a big load on his back. It contained varieties of foodstuffs like rice, dhal, spices, oil, flour, and cooking utensils. The boy claimed to be a disciple of her husband who had sent him to deliver these goods to his house. The surprised wife told the boy that her husband had no disciples, so it was not possible that he had sent him with all these items. But the boy insisted, repeating that her husband was his guru and had sent him to deliver these items to his house.

The boy further told her that her husband had become disturbed with him for carrying the load so slowly and had thus beaten him. Indeed, he raised his cloth and showed the *brāhmaṇa's* wife the marks on his back. She became surprised that her husband could be so cruel as to beat such a young and beautiful boy. She told him to sit inside the house so she could cook something and offer him some *prasada*.

Later that day, the *brāhmaṇa* returned home empty handed. He was feeling very dejected because he and his wife would have to fast. As soon as his wife saw him, she began scolding him for having made the young boy carry such a heavy load and for beating him for not carrying it swiftly. The *brāhmaṇa* was confused by his wife's behavior. She had never spoken to him like this before and he had no idea what she was talking about. He asked her to explain and she told him what had happened. She said that the boy was still in the house, but when the *brāhmaṇa* searched for him, he was nowhere to be found.

Later, as he sat to read his *Bhagavad-gita* he found that the verse he had crossed out was again intact—the red ink was gone. He started weeping, realizing that the young boy was actually Krishna who had indeed come to his house to fulfill the pledge He made in the *Bhagavad-gita*—that He carries and delivers the needs of His devotees. The *brāhmaṇa* lamented that he was not as fortunate as his wife who had been able to see Krishna personally and he condemned himself for doubting the words of *Bhagavad-gita*.

As mentioned earlier, Krishna's words are nondifferent from Him, so the *brāhmaṇa's* striking out the verse amounted to striking Krishna's body. The scratches and blood on the boy's back represented the red ink the *brāhmaṇa* had used to cross out the verse.

Lord Krishna says in the *Gita*:

> *yaḥ śāstra-vidhim utsṛjya, vartate kāma-kārataḥ*
> *na sa siddhim avāpnoti, na sukhaṁ na parāṁ gatim*

> "He who discards scriptural injunctions and acts according to his own whims attains neither perfection, nor happiness, nor the supreme destination."

The way of perfection in godly life or Krishna consciousness is to have firm faith in the words of the Supreme Lord and the authorized teachers.

This current edition of *Gita-Mahatmya* is a polished version of what was presented earlier. More scriptural references have been added to increase the sweetness. It is my sincere wish that the readers will delve more deeply into the mysteries of *Bhagavad-gita* and thus attain the ultimate goal of life: love of God.

Isvara Dasa
(Completed on the appearance day of Lord Nityananda.
Vrindavan Dhama,
February 9, 1998).

The Glories of Chapter One

Parvati said: My dear husband, you know all the transcendental truths, and by your mercy I have heard the glories of the Supreme Personality of Godhead, Lord Krishna. Oh Lord, now I long to hear from you the glories of the *Srimad Bhagavad-gita*, which was spoken by Lord Krishna, and by hearing which, one's devotion to Lord Krishna increases.

Lord Siva replied: That person, whose body is the color of a dark rain cloud, whose carrier is the king of birds (Garuda) and who is lying on Ananta-Sesa (the thousand-headed serpent), that Lord Vishnu, whose glories have no limit, I am always worshiping.

My dear Parvati, once, after Lord Vishnu had killed the demon Mura, He was resting peacefully on Ananta-Sesa, when the bestower of all good fortune of the universe, Sri Lakshmi, respectfully inquired from Him. She said: Bhagavan, You are the controller and maintainer of the whole universe, but yet You are sleeping unhappily on this ocean of milk. What is the reason?

Lord Vishnu said: My dear Lakshmi, I am not sleeping, but I am watching how wonderfully My energy is working. It is by this wonderful energy of Mine that I am controlling all things, and yet I remain separate. And it is by remembering these divine activities of Mine that the great devotees and yogis manage to free themselves from the wheel of birth and death, and attain the transcendental nature of Mine, which is eternal and free from all qualities.

Lakshmi said: O controller of all things. You are the goal of the meditation of great yogis. Nothing can go on without You. And yet You are separate. You are the cause of creation, maintenance, and destruction of all the material universes. Kindly inform me about the workings of Your wonderful energies, which are so attractive, that even You are lying here, meditating upon them.

Lord Vishnu said: My dear Lakshmi, the workings of My multifold energies, and how to become free from the bonds of birth and death, and attain My eternal nature can only be understood by one of pure intelligence, who has an inclination to render service unto Me. This transcendental knowledge is fully explained in the *Srimad Bhagavad-gita.*

Lakshmi said: My dear Lord, if You Yourself are amazed by the workings of Your energies, and are ever trying to fathom their limit, then how is it possible that the *Bhagavad-gita* can describe those unlimited energies of Yours, how to cross over them, and how to attain the transcendental nature?

Lord Vishnu said: I Myself have manifested in the form of the *Bhagavad-gita*. Please understand that the first five chapters are My five heads, the next ten chapters are My ten arms, and the sixteenth chapter is My stomach. The last two chapters are My lotus feet. In this way you should understand the transcendental Deity of the *Bhagavad-gita*. This *Bhagavad-gita* is the destroyer of all sins. And an intelligent person who daily recites one chapter or even one sloka, one half sloka, or at least one quarter sloka, will attain the same position as Susharma had attained.

Lakshmi asked: Who was Susharma? What class did he belong to? And what destination did he attain?

Lord Vishnu said: My dear Lakshmi, Susharma was a very wicked and a most sinful man. Although he was born in a *brahmana* family, his family had no Vedic knowledge. And he took pleasure only from hurting others. He never engaged in the chanting of My names, in giving charity, or receiving guests. In fact, he never performed any pious activities. For his livelihood he collected leaves, and sold them in the bazaar. He especially enjoyed drinking wine, and eating flesh. In this way he passed his life.

One day that foolish Susharma went to the garden of a sage to collect leaves, when a snake came and bit him, and he died. After his death he was cast into many hells, where he suffered for a long time. Then he attained the body of a bull. The bull was purchased by a crippled man, who engaged him in his service. For about seven or eight years he was carrying extremely heavy loads. One day the crippled man piled a very heavy load onto the back of his bull. He was forcing the bull along quickly, when suddenly the bull fell over and became unconscious. Many persons gathered there to see what was happening. Feeling sorry for the bull, a pious man bestowed upon the bull the results of some of his pious activities. Seeing that, other persons standing there started remembering their pious activities, and offered the results of some of those activities to the bull. In the crowd there was also a prostitute who did not know if she had ever performed any pious activities, but seeing everyone else offering their pious credits to the bull, she also offered the results of any pious activities she might have performed. After that, the bull died, and was taken to the abode of Yamaraja, the god of death.

There, Yamaraja informed him, "You are now free from the reactions of all your previous sinful deeds, due to the pious credits given to you by the prostitute." Then he took birth in a very high *brahmana* family. In that birth, he was able to remember his past lives. After many days, he decided to search out the prostitute, who had been the cause of freeing him from his hellish situation.

After he found and introduced himself to the prostitute, he inquired from her, "What were the pious activities performed by you, the fruits of which freed me from my hellish situation?" The prostitute replied, "My dear sir, in that cage is a parrot, which recites something everyday. Hearing that recitation my heart has become completely pure. The results of hearing that recitation I had given to you." Thereafter they both inquired from the parrot about the recitation.

The parrot, remembering his previous life, started to narrate his history. He said, "Previously, I had been a learned *brahmana*, but due to my pride, I used to insult other learned persons. I was also extremely jealous. After I died, I was cast into many hells, and after a long time of suffering, I achieved this body of a parrot. Due to my past sinful activities, my mother and father died while I was a baby. One day, while I was lying on the hot sands with no protection some *rishis* saw me, and took me to their ashram, and put me in a cage. At that place, the children of the *rishis* were learning the recitation of the first chapter of the *Srimad Bhagavad-gita.* Hearing them repeat the *slokas*, I also started repeating those *slokas* along with them. Shortly after, a thief stole me from there and sold me to this pious lady."

Lord Vishnu continued: By reciting the first chapter of the *Bhagavad-gita,* the parrot became completely pure. And by hearing the recitation, the prostitute also became completely pure. And by receiving some of the pious results of hearing the recitation, Susharma also became completely pure.

After discussing for some time the glories of the first chapter of the *Bhagavad-gita,* Susharma returned to his home, and the three of them individually engaged in reciting the first chapter of the *Srimad Bhagavad-gita,* and quickly attained the supreme destination, Vaikuntha.

Anyone who recites, hears, or studies the first chapter of the *Bhagavad-gita* will very easily cross over the ocean of material miseries and attain the service of the lotus feet of Lord Krishna.

The Glories of Chapter Two

Lord Vishnu said: My dear Lakshmi, you have heard from Me the glories of the first chapter of the *Bhagavad-gita.* Now please listen carefully, as I tell you the glories of the second chapter.

Once, in the South, in the town of Pandharpur, a learned *brahmana* by the name of Devashyama lived. He was able to perform all kinds of fire sacrifices. He also knew the importance of receiving guest. And by his activities he managed to satisfy all the demigods. But he was not happy and peaceful in his heart and mind. He had a desire to attain knowledge of the soul's relationship with the Supersoul, Paramatma. Towards this end he would invite many *yogis* and *tapasvis*, render all kinds of service to them, and inquire from them about the Absolute Truth. In this way he passed many years of his life.

One day, while he was walking, he saw a yogi sitting cross-legged with his eyes fixed on the tip of his nose, totally absorbed in meditation. Devashyama could perceive that this yogi was completely peaceful, and without any material desires. Devashyama, with the greatest respect and reverence, fell at the feet of the yogi, and inquired from him, how he could attain complete peace of mind. At that time, the yogi, who had complete knowledge of the Supreme Personality of Godhead, Lord Krishna, advised Devashyama to go to the village of Sowpur and meet Mitravan, a goat-herder, and take instructions in the science of God-realization from him. After hearing this, Devashyama again and again offered his respectful obeisances at the feet of the yogi and then left for Sowpur. When he arrived there, he found on the northern side, a beautiful forest where Mitravan lived. When he entered the forest, he saw Mitravan sitting on top of some rocks on the bank of a small river.

Mitravan looked very beautiful and totally peaceful. In the forest the wind was blowing very gently and a beautiful aroma was emanating from every direction. The goats were peacefully moving here and there—totally unafraid. Some were seen to be sitting next to tigers and other ferocious animals.

When Devashyama saw this scene, his mind became peaceful, and he respectfully approached Mitravan and sat close to him. Mitravan appeared to be fully absorbed in his meditation. After some time Devashyama inquired from him how he would be able to attain devotion to Lord Krishna. When Mitravan heard this question, for a moment, he was lost in deep thought. Then he replied, "My dear learned Devashyama, once long ago, I was in the forest looking after the goats, when a very ferocious tiger attacked. All the goats ran here and there to save themselves. I also ran off, due to fear of the tiger. From some distance I looked back and saw that the tiger on the bank of this river had caught one of my goats. At that time a strange and wonderful thing happened. The tiger lost all his anger and desire to eat my goat. Thereupon, my goat asked the tiger, 'You have attained your food, so why are you not eating the meat of my body? You should immediately kill me, and with great relish eat up my flesh. Why are you hesitating?'

"The tiger said, 'My dear goat, since I have come to this place, all anger has left me, and I have no hunger or thirst.' The goat said, 'I also do not know why I am feeling so fearless and peaceful. What can be the reason for this? If you know, then kindly inform me.' The tiger replied, 'I also do not know. Let us inquire from that person.'

"When I saw this exchange between the tiger and goat I became very much astonished. At that time they approached me, and inquired as to the reason. I noticed a monkey sitting on the branch of a nearby tree. I went with the two of them and inquired from the monkey.

"With great respect the monkey said, 'Listen, I will tell you a very old story. In this forest, just in front of you, there is a very large temple in which Lord Brahma installed a Sivalinga. Long ago, a learned sage of the name Sukama, who had performed many austerities, lived there. Daily he would bring flowers from the forest and water from the river, and worship Lord Siva.

"'In this way, he was living here for many years, when one day a sage arrived. At that time, Sukama brought fruits and water and fed the sage. After the sage had eaten and rested, Sukama said that he was living here, performing austerities and worship, only to obtain knowledge of Lord Krishna. But the results of his austerities had been attained today by coming in contact with him.

"'When the sage heard the words of Sukama, which were full of submission, he became greatly pleased. And he wrote the second chapter of the *Srimad Bhagavad-gita* on a stone. He instructed Sukama to daily read those verses and told him that by so doing, he would quickly attain his goal. After having spoken thus, the sage disappeared from that place while Sukama was looking on. After that, following the instructions of the sage, Sukama recited those verses daily for the rest of his life. Quickly he attained complete knowledge of Lord Krishna. And from the day he started reciting those verses, he felt no more thirst or hunger.

"'And due to his austerities and devotion performed at this place, anyone who visits here does not feel the pangs of hunger and thirst, and immediately attains complete peace.'"

Mitravan said, "My dear Devashyama, after the monkey had finished telling us that wonderful story, I, along with the tiger and goat, went to that temple. There we found the second chapter of the *Srimad Bhagavad-gita* written on a stone. And we started to recite those verses daily. In this way, we were soon able to attain devotion to Lord Krishna. My dear *brahmana*, if you also start reciting the verses of the second chapter of the *Srimad Bhagavad-gita,* you will quickly attain the mercy of Lord Krishna."

Lord Vishnu said: My dear Lakshmi, in this way Devashyama attained knowledge from Mitravan and after worshipping that great soul, he returned to Pandharpur and daily recited the second chapter. He would also recite it to anyone who visited Pandharpur. In this way Devashyama attained the lotus feet of Lord Krishna. My dear Lakshmi, these are the glories of the second chapter of the *Srimad Bhagavad-gita*.

The Glories of Chapter Three

Lord Vishnu said: My dear Lakshmi, in the town of Janasthan was a *brahmana* called Jada, who was born in the dynasty of Kaushik. Jada gave up the religious activities enjoined in the *shastras* which are to be followed by the *brahmana* class and took to many irreligious activities. He was very fond of gambling, drinking, hunting, and visiting prostitutes. Having wasted his wealth, he went to the northern countries on a business trip. While there, he gained much wealth and decided to return to Janasthan. One day, having traveled a long distance, he found himself in a very deserted place. As the sun set and everywhere became engulfed by darkness, he decided to take rest for the night under a tree. While he was resting, some robbers came, beat him to death, and stole his wealth. Because Jada had given up all religious activities and led a sinful life, after his death he attained the form of a ghost.

The son of Jada was very religious and learned in the Vedic *shastras*. When he saw that his father had not returned to Janasthan after a long time, he decided to go and search for him. For many days he traveled here and there in search of his father, and whenever he met any travelers he would inquire from them about his father. One day, he met a person who knew his father and informed him of the events that had taken place. When Jada's son heard the news of his father's death, he decided to go to Kasi (Banaras) to offer pinda (worship) for the release of his father from his hellish condition. On the ninth day of his journey, he happened to take rest under the same tree under which his father had been killed. At that place, in the evening, he performed his daily worship to Lord Krishna, and he also recited the third chapter of the *Srimad Bhagavad-gita*. As he completed his recitation, a loud sound came from the sky. When he looked up, he saw his father there, and in front of his eyes, his father's form changed into one of the most beautiful beings, who had four hands, and was wearing a yellow dhoti. His body was the color of a dark rain cloud and his bodily effulgence was lighting up all the directions. His father offered his blessing to him. The son inquired as to the meaning of these wonderful happenings. The father said, "My dear son, you recited the third chapter of the *Srimad Bhagavad-gita*, and thus freed me from the ghost form which I had received due to my sinful activities. Now you should return to your home, because the purpose for which you were traveling to Kasi (Banaras) has been achieved by your reciting the third chapter of the *Bhagavad-gita*."

When the son asked if there were any further instructions, the father said, "My brother also had led a very sinful life and he is suffering somewhere in the darkest regions of hell. So if you wish to free him and our other ancestors, who are suffering here and there, in different species in the material universe, then kindly recite the third chapter of the *Srimad Bhagavad-gita*. And by that recitation they will all attain a form similar to Lord Vishnu's, and go to Vaikuntha."

When the son heard the father's instructions he replied, "If that is the case, then I will recite the third chapter until all the souls who are trapped in hellish life are freed." At that time his father blessed him with the words, "Let it be." Then an airplane arrived from the spiritual world of Vaikuntha and took the father to his destination.

Thereafter, the son returned to Janasthan and sat in front of the Deity of Lord Krishna. With a desire to free all conditioned souls from hellish life, he started reciting the third chapter of the *Srimad Bhagavad-gita*. While his recitation was continuing day after day, Lord Vishnu sent His messengers, the Vishnudutas, to the kingdom of Yamaraja. Yamaraja is in charge of administering punishment to the sinful living entities. When the Vishnudutas arrived in front of Yamaraja, they informed him, that they had a message from Lord Vishnu, who is lying on the bed of Ananta-Sesa in the ocean of milk.

They told him that Lord Vishnu inquired as to his welfare and also ordered him to free all the conditioned souls who were suffering in hell.

When Yamaraja heard this instruction from Lord Vishnu, he immediately had all of the conditioned souls released from hell and then personally went with those Vishnudutas to the ocean of milk, known as Svetadwipa, to have the *darshan* of Lord Vishnu. When he arrived there, he saw Lord Vishnu, lying on the bed of Ananta-Sesa. His body had the effulgence of suns, and Lakshmi-Devi, the goddess of fortune, was massaging His feet. He was surrounded on all sides by rishis, sages, and demigods headed by Lord Indra, who were all singing the praises of Lord Vishnu. Lord Brahma was also present, reciting the *Vedas.* Yamaraja fell down and offered his respects before Lord Vishnu, and offered the following praise, "My dear Vishnu, You are the well-wisher of all the conditioned souls. There is no limit of Your glories. From You the *Vedas* have come, You are time, and in the course of time You will destroy all things. You are the cause and maintainer of the three worlds and You are the Supersoul in everyone's heart, directing the activities of living beings. You are the guru of the whole universe, and the goal of all devotees. Oh, lotus-eyed one, please accept my obeisances again and again. Your glories are unlimited."

In this way Yamaraja with folded hands offered his respects to Lord Vishnu. Yamaraja continued, "As per Your instructions, I have released all the conditioned souls from hell. So kindly instruct me, what work You wish me to perform now." Lord Vishnu replied in a voice as deep as thunder and as sweet as nectar, "My dear Dharmaraja [Yamaraja], you are equal to everyone, and I do not need to instruct you on your duties. Kindly return to your abode with my full blessings and continue your duty." At that time, Lord Vishnu disappeared from the vision of Yamaraja, and Yamaraja returned to his own abode.

When the *brahmana,* Jada's son had successfully freed all his ancestors and the rest of the conditioned souls from hell, the Vishnudutas came and took him to the abode of Lord Vishnu. There he engaged in the service of the lotus feet of the Supreme Personality of Godhead eternally.

The Glories of Chapter Four

Lord Vishnu said: My dear Lakshmi, now I will describe the glories of the fourth chapter of the *Srimad Bhagavad-gita*.

On the bank of the river Ganges at Kasi (Banaras) is the temple of Vishvanath, where a great saint called Bharat lived. Daily, with the greatest devotion, he would recite the fourth chapter of *Srimad Bhagavad-gita*. Previously, when Bharat had been traveling on pilgrimage he had gone to the town of Tapodan to take *darshan* of the Deity of Lord Krishna. On leaving that town, he saw two bael fruit trees. Deciding to take rest under the shade of those trees, he lay down, using the root of one of the tree as a pillow and the root of the other to rest his feet on.

When Bharat left from that place, the two trees started to dry up. Within five or six days both trees completely dried up and died. The two souls who had been living in those trees took their next birth as the daughters of a pious *brahmana*. When the girls were seven years old, they were taken on pilgrimage to Kasi (Banaras). While wandering in Kasi, they happened to see the great sage Bharat. When they saw Bharat they immediately went and fell at his feet and in sweet words said, "O Maharaja Bharat, due to your mercy we both became freed from the tree form of life." When Bharat Maharaja heard their statement he became surprised. He inquired from them, "My dear daughters, where and when did I come in contact with you, and free you from the form of trees? Also kindly inform me how you attained the form of trees because I do not know anything of this matter."

The girls first told Bharat Maharaja the reason for their attaining the form of trees. One of the girls said, "Maharaja, on the bank of the river Godavari there is a sacred place known as Chinnapaap. At that place, there was a *rishi* called Sachatapa. He was performing very great and difficult austerities. In the hot season he would sit in between many fires, and in the cold season, he would stand in the cold river. In the course of time, he became completely pure, and had complete control of his senses, and slowly he attained the lotus feet of the Supreme Personality of Godhead, Lord Krishna. Lord Brahma went daily to take the *darshan* of Sachatapa and put questions before him about the devotional service of Lord Krishna. Lord Indra meanwhile, became worried seeing the elevated position of Sachatapa. He thought that Sachatapa might one day usurp his position as the king of heaven. At that time, Lord Indra called the two of us, who in that birth were apsaras in the heavenly kingdom, and instructed us, 'Go and cause the fall down of Sachatapa, before he tries to usurp me from my position.'

"After receiving Lord Indra's instructions, we went to the bank of the Godavari River where Sachatapa was performing austerities. We started to sing and dance very provocatively close to Sachatapa, with the intention of causing him to engage in a sexual relationship with us. While dancing, our covering cloth slipped down and our breasts became visible. At that time, taking water in his hand, that sage cursed us. He said. 'Both of you go and become bael trees on the bank of the river Ganga.' Upon hearing his curse, we fell at his feet, begged his forgiveness, and explained that we were simply the servants of Lord Indra. Seeing our submissive attitude the sage became pleased and informed us that we would remain as trees until Maharaja Bharat came in contact with us. And he also blessed us that we would be able to remember our previous births.

"My dear Maharaja Bharat when you visited Tapodan, you rested beneath us when we were in the form of bael trees. You recited the fourth chapter of the *Srimad Bhagavad-gita,* and by hearing that recitation, we not only became free from that tree form of life and attained birth in a devotee family, but we also lost all desire for enjoying in this material world."

Lord Vishnu said: My dear Lakshmi, when those two girls recited their history before Bharat Maharaja, he became very happy, and left for his *ashram*. The two girls throughout their life, carefully recited the fourth chapter of the *Srimad Bhagavad-gita* daily and attained devotion to My lotus feet.

The Glories of Chapter Five

Lord Vishnu said: Now I will describe to you the unlimited glories of the fifth chapter of the *Bhagavad-gita.* Listen very carefully.

In the state of Madra, there is a town of the name Puru Kutsapur. There, lived the *brahmana,* Pingala. During his childhood he was trained in various *brahminical* activities and was taught the *Vedas.* But he had no interest in his studies. When he reached his youth he gave up his *brahminical* pursuits and started to learn to play instruments as well as singing and dancing. Slowly he became so famous in this field that the king himself invited him to live in the palace. While he was living there he slowly degraded more and more into sinful life. He started to enjoy with other men's wives and engage in all kinds of sinful activities and intoxication.

He became so proud of his position as he gained more and more intimacy with the king. He especially enjoyed criticizing others to the king in private. Pingala's wife, Aruna, was born in a low-class family. She was very lusty and enjoyed relationships with many men. When her husband found out about her activities, she decided to kill him. Late one night she chopped off his head and buried his body in the garden. After his death Pingala fell into the deepest regions of hell and after having suffered there for a long time he took birth as a vulture. Aruna, after freely enjoying with many men contacted venereal disease and her youthful body very soon became ugly and unattractive. When she died she went on to hell and after having suffered for a long time, she attained the body of a female parrot.

One day the parrot was searching here and there for food. In the meantime the vulture, who in his previous life had been Pingala, saw the female parrot, remembered his last life, and understood that this parrot had been his wife. He attacked her with his sharp beak. The parrot fell down into the water contained in a human skull and drowned. Just then a hunter came and shot the vulture with an arrow. The vulture fell and his head also dropped into the water of that skull and he drowned.

Then the messengers of Yamaraja came and took them to the abode of death. They became very afraid remembering their past sinful lives. When they came in front of Yamaraja he told them, "You are now free of all sins and you may go to Vaikuntha." Pingala and Aruna askedYamaraja how two sinful persons, such as they, had attained the right to go to Vaikuntha.

Yamaraja replied, "On the banks of the river Ganga lived a great devotee of Lord Vishnu called Vat. He was free from lust and greed. Daily he recited the fifth chapter of the *Bhagavad-gita* and when Vat gave up his body he went straight to Vaikuntha. Due to his daily reciting the fifth chapter of the *Bhagavad-gita*, his body became completely pure, and because of your coming in contact with the skull of his body you both have attained Vaikuntha. This is the glory of the fifth chapter of the *Bhagavad-gita.*"

Lord Vishnu said: My dear Lakshmi, when they both heard the glories of the *Bhagavad-gita* from Yamaraja they became very happy and sat down in the flower airplane which had come to take them to Vaikuntha.

Anyone who hears the fifth chapter of the *Bhagavad-gita,* even the most sinful, will attain Vaikuntha.

The Glories of Chapter Six

Lord Vishnu said: Now I will tell you the glories of the sixth chapter of the *Srimad Bhagavad-gita*. Whoever hears this description, will be liberated from the material world.

On the bank of the Godavari river, there is a beautiful town called Pratishthanpur (Paithan), where I am famous by the name Pippalesh. In that town there was a king named Janshruti, whom the people loved very much and whose qualities were unlimited. He performed daily fire sacrifices, which were so opulent and large that the smoke from them reached the heavenly pleasure garden known as Nandanvan, and made the leaves of the kalpavriksa trees black. The trees appeared to be offering respects to King Janshruti. Due to the pious activities of the king, demigods always resided in Pratishthanpur.

When Janshruti gave in charity, he would distribute just like the clouds distribute rain. And due to his pure religious activities, the rain always came at the right time. The fields were always full of crops, which were not disturbed by the six types of rodents. He regularly dug wells and lakes for the welfare of the citizens.

The demigods, being very pleased with Janshruti, went to his palace in the form of swans to bless him. They were flying through the sky, one behind the other, talking together. Bhadrashva, along with two or three other swans, flew ahead of the rest. At that time, the other swans addressed Bhadrashva, "Oh, brother, why are you flying ahead? Do you not see in front of you the great King Janshruti, who is so powerful that he can burn up his enemies by his desire." When Bhadrashva heard the words of the other swans, he started to laugh and said, "Oh brothers, is this King Janshruti as powerful as the great sage Raikva?"

When the king heard the words of the swans, he immediately came down from the roof of his high palace and happily sat on his throne. He sent for his chariot driver, Maha, and instructed him to go and find the great sage Raikva. When the chariot driver, Maha heard the king's instructions, he became very happy, and left immediately to search out Raikva. First he traveled to Kashipuri, where Lord Vishvanath resides for the welfare of all beings. Next, he went to Gaya, where the lotus-eyed Lord Gadadhara, who is capable of freeing all beings from the bondage of birth and death, stays. After having traveled to many holy places, Maha came to Mathura, which is capable of destroying all sins. In this place the Supreme Personality of Godhead, Lord Krishna, resides. All the great sages, the demigods, the *Vedas,* and other *shastras* in their personal forms, perform austerities and render service to Lord Krishna. Mathura which is in the shape of a half-moon, and is situated on the bank of the beautiful devotion-giving River Yamuna. In that area is the beautiful Govardhana hill, which adds to the splendor and glory of Mathura-Mandala like a large jewel in a crown. It is surrounded by pure trees and creepers. There are also twelve wonderful forests surrounding Mathura in which Lord Krishna enjoys His wonderful pastimes.

After leaving Mathura, Maha traveled to the West, and then to the North. One day, he came to a town known as Kashmir in which he saw a very large and shining white place. All the people, even the foolish men, looked as beautiful as demigods because many sacrificial fires were burning continuously. It looked as if a row of clouds always hung over the town. The Deity of Lord Siva, known as Manikeshvara, resided there. The king of Kashmir had just returned from defeating many kings, and was engaged in worshipping Lord Siva. Due to his great devotion to Lord Siva, that king was known as Manikeshvar. Just close to the door of the temple, sitting on a small cart underneath a tree, Maha saw the great sage Raikva. When he recognized Raikva from the description of Janshruti, he immediately fell at his feet and asked him, "Oh, great sage, where do you live? And what is your full name? You are such a highly elevated person. Why are you sitting in this place?" When Raikva heard the words of Maha, he thought for some time, and then replied, "I am fully satisfied, I do not require anything."

When Maha heard this reply, in his heart he could understand everything. He immediately left on the long journey back to Pratishthanpur. When he reached his destination, he immediately went and offered his respects to the king, and with folded hands informed the king of all the events which had taken place. After the king had heard everything from Maha he decided to leave at once, to take the *darshan* of the great sage Raikva. Sitting in a beautiful chariot, and taking with him many valuable gifts, he left for Kashmir. When he reached the place where the sage Raikva was staying, he fell at his feet and placed the valuable silks and jewels before him. The great sage Raikva became angry. He said, "O foolish king, take all these useless things and put them in your chariot, and leave from this place." The king, with great devotion, fell at the feet of Raikva, and begged his forgiveness, asking him to be merciful upon him. He asked, "O sage, how have you attained such a high state of renunciation and devotion to the Lord?"

Becoming pleased with the king's submissive attitude, Raikva replied "Daily I recite the sixth chapter of the *Srimad Bhagavad-gita.*"

After that, King Janshruti heard from Raikva the sixth chapter of the *Srimad Bhagavad-gita*. Thereafter, he engaged in daily reciting it. In due course of time a flower airplane arrived and took him to Vaikuntha. Meanwhile, the great sage, Raikva, continued reciting the sixth chapter of the *Srimad Bhagavad-gita* daily. Then he also went to Vaikuntha, where he engaged in the service of the lotus feet of the Supreme Lord Vishnu.

Anyone, who recites the sixth chapter of the *Srimad Bhagavad-gita*, will very soon attain service to the lotus feet of Lord Vishnu. Of this there is no doubt.

The Glories of Chapter Seven

Lord Siva said: My dear Parvati, now I will tell you the glories of the seventh chapter of the *Srimad Bhagavad-gita.* Hearing which, one feels his ears have been filled with divine nectar.

Pataliputra is the name of a large town, which has many large gates. In that town lived a *brahmana* of the name Shankukarna. He was a businessman, and had amassed a very large wealth. He had never performed any type of devotional activities, nor had he performed the necessary ritualistic performances for the sake of his forefathers. He became so rich that even great kings would dine at his house. Shankukarna was also the most miserly of persons, and he kept his wealth buried under the ground.

Once, when Shankukarna was going with his children and other relatives to attend his fourth marriage, he stopped at one place to rest for the night. While he was sleeping, a snake came and bit him. His sons and relatives called for doctors and mantra chanters, but no one was able to help Shankukarna, and soon he died.

After death he attained the body of a Preta-Sarp, a snake-ghost. The only thing he was able to think about was his wealth, which was buried close to the house where he had lived. He had not even told his own family of the whereabouts of his wealth. In the form of a Preta-Sarp he resided at the place where his wealth was buried, so that no one else could take it. After some time he became tired of being trapped in the form of a Preta-Sarp and he appeared to his sons in dreams and requested them to help him. In the morning, when his lazy sons woke up, they told each other about the dream they had seen. One of his sons took a large spade in his hands and went to the place where the father had indicated he was living. When he reached that place he realized that he was not aware of the exact spot where the wealth was buried. The son was exceptionally greedy, and he searched for a long time, until he came across a snake hole, which he promptly started to dig out.

Soon a large and fearful-looking snake came out of that hole and said, "O fool, who are you? Why have you come here? Who has sent you? And why are you digging at this place? Reply to my questions at once."

The son replied, "I am your son. My name is Siva. In a dream last night I saw that there were hidden treasures buried at this place and I came to take them." When he heard Siva's words the Preta-Sarp started to laugh and said, "If you are my son, then why are you not performing the necessary rituals to free me from this hellish situation. Due to greed in my last life, I attained this body and now you are heading the same way."

The son asked, "My dear father, kindly tell me how you can be freed from this hellish situation?" The Preta-Sarp said, "Not by any kind of charity, *tapasya* or *yajna*. Only by the recitation of the seventh chapter of the *Bhagavad-gita* will I be freed from the wheel of birth and death. My dear son kindly perform the *shraddha* ceremony and on that day, invite a *brahmana* who is in the habit of chanting the seventh chapter of the *Bhagavad-gita* and feed him very sumptuously."

Siva, along with his other brother fulfilled the instructions of their father and while the *brahmana* was chanting the seventh chapter of the *Srimad Bhagavad-gita,* Sankukarna gave up that frightful body of a Preta-Sarp and attained a divine four-armed body. He blessed his sons and informed them where his wealth was and then he left for Vaikuntha.

His sons, whose minds had become fixed in devotion to Lord Krishna, used that wealth for building temples, digging wells, and distributing foodstuffs. They engaged daily in the recitation of the seventh chapter of the *Srimad Bhagavad-gita* and quickly they attained the lotus feet of Lord Krishna.

Lord Siva said: My dear Parvati, I have told you the wonderful glories of the seventh chapter of the *Bhagavad-gita*. Anyone, who hears this description, will be freed from all sinful reactions.

The Glories of Chapter Eight

Lord Siva said: My dear Parvati, now please listen to the glories of the eighth chapter of the *Srimad Bhagavad-gita*. After listening to this, you will feel great joy.

In the South in the town Amardhkapur lived a *brahmana* called Bhavasharma who had married a prostitute. He enjoyed eating meat, drinking wine, stealing, going with other's wives, and hunting. One day, that sinful Bhavasharma was invited to a party, where he drank so much alcohol that it started to come out of his mouth. After the party, he became very sick and suffered from chronic dysentery, and after many days of suffering he died and attained the body of a date palm tree.

One day, two *brahma-rakshasas* (ghosts) came and took shelter under that tree. Their previous life story was as follows:

There was a *brahmana* named Kushibal, who was learned in the *Vedas* and had studied all branches of knowledge. His wife's name was Kumati and she was evil-minded. Although that *brahmana* was learned, he was also greedy. Along with his wife, he used to collect lots of charity everyday, but he would never give charity to any other *brahmana*. When their time came to die, they attained the forms of *brahma-rakshasas*. As *brahma-rakshasas*, they continuously wandered here and there over the earth suffering from hunger and thirst. One day they rested under that date palm tree.

At that time, the wife asked her husband, "How can we get free from this curse of being *brahma-rakshasas*?" He replied, "By knowledge of Brahman, by knowledge of the self, by knowledge of fruitive activities. Without such knowledge it is not possible to get free from our sinful reactions." Upon hearing this, the wife asked, "*Kim tad brahma kim adhyatmam kim karma purusottama,* O my Lord, what is Brahman, What is the self? What are fruitive activities?" Completely by accident, the wife happened to chant half of the first sloka of the eighth chapter of the *Srimad Bhagavad-gita*. At that time, having heard this half sloka, Bhavasharma broke free from the form of a tree, and again attained the body of a *brahmana*—completely free from all sin. Suddenly from the sky came a flower airplane, which took the husband and wife back home, back to Godhead, Vaikuntha.

Afterwards, the *brahmana*, Bhavasharma, with great respect, wrote down that half *sloka (kim tad brahma kim adhyatmam kim karma purusottama).* With the intention of worshiping Lord Krishna, he went to Kashipuri and started performing great austerities, while continually chanting that half *sloka*.

Meanwhile in Vaikuntha, Lakshmi seeing Lord Vishnu, had risen suddenly from taking rest, inquired with folded hands, "Why have You risen so suddenly from Your sleep?" Lord Vishnu said, "My dear Lakshmi, in Kashipuri, on the bank of the river Ganges, my devotee is performing great austerities continually chanting half a *sloka* of the eighth chapter of the *Srimad Bhagavad-gita*. For a long time I have been thinking how to award his devotion."

Parvati asked Lord Siva: When Lord Vishnu was so pleased with His devotee, what benediction did He bestow upon him?

Lord Siva said: Bhavasharma went to Vaikuntha, to engage in the eternal service of the lotus feet of Lord Vishnu. Not only that, but all of his ancestors also attained the lotus feet of Lord Vishnu.

My dear Parvati, I have described to you just a little of the glories of the eighth chapter of the *Srimad Bhagavad-gita.*

THE GLORIES OF CHAPTER NINE

Lord Siva said: My dear Parvati, now I will relate to you the glories of the ninth chapter of the *Srimad Bhagavad-gita*.

There was a town of the name Mahismati on the bank of the Narmada River, where a *brahmana* called Madhava lived. That *brahmana* very strictly followed all the injunctions of the *Vedas,* and possessed all the good qualities of the *brahminical* class. Due to his being so learned, he would receive a lot of charity, and with his accumulated wealth he started to perform a great fire sacrifice. He bought a goat for offering in sacrifice, and when they started to cleanse the goat in preparation for it's sacrifice, to everyone's great surprise, the goat started to laugh. In a loud voice the goat said, "O *brahmana*, what is the benefit of performing many fire sacrifices that simply bind us up in the wheel of birth and death. Just see my position due to my performing so many fire sacrifices."

When everyone who was gathered there heard the words of the goat, they became curious, and with folded hands, the *brahmana* asked, "How did you become a goat? In your previous life, which caste did you belong to and what activities did you perform?" The goat replied, "O *brahmana*, in my previous birth I was born in a very pure *brahmana* family and I very carefully performed all the ritualistic activities enjoined in the *Vedas.* One day my wife wished to worship Durga, so that our child might be cured of his disease. For this purpose she requested me to bring a goat. When we sacrificed the goat at the temple of Mother Durga, the goat cursed me, 'O sinful, lowest of all, you wish to make my children fatherless. For this reason you will also take birth as a goat.' O *brahmana,* O Madhava, when the time for my death came I attained this body of a goat but by the grace of Lord Govinda I can remember my previous births. If you wish to hear one other interesting story then I will tell you.

"In the place known as Kuruksetra which is capable of giving liberation, there once lived a king called Chandrasharma, who was in the dynasty of the sun-god. Once, at the time of the solar eclipse, the king wished to give charity to a *brahmana*. Included in the charity was a sudra, whose body was completely black. The king, accompanied by his priest took bath in a sacred lake, put on clean cloth, applied sandalwood, and returned to his place. With devotion he gave charity to a qualified *brahmana*. Suddenly, from the black sudra's heart, a sinful *chandala* (dog-eater) appeared and after a little while, a female *chandala* also appeared from that black sudra's body. The *chandalas* went towards the *brahmana* and entered into his body. The *brahmana* remained undisturbed and started to chant the ninth chapter of the *Srimad Bhagavad-gita,* while remembering Lord Govinda. The king witnessing all these activities was stunned, unable to say anything. As soon as the words of the ninth chapter of the *Srimad Bhagavad-gita* came on the lips of the *brahmana*, the Vishnudutas appeared there and chased away the two *chandalas*.

"The king inquired from the *brahmana*, 'O learned one, who were those two persons and which mantra did you chant? Which deity did you remember?' The *brahmana* replied, 'Sin personified appeared in the form of the *chandala,* along with offense personified in the form of the female *chandala.* At that time I started chanting the ninth chapter of the *Srimad Bhagavad-gita*, which is capable of releasing one from all fearful situations. By reciting the ninth chapter of the *Srimad Bhagavad-gita*, I am always able to remember the lotus feet of Lord Govinda.' Upon hearing this the king learned the chanting of the ninth chapter of the *Srimad Bhagavad-gita* from the *brahmana*. Gradually he managed to attain the lotus feet of Lord Govinda."

When Madhava heard this discourse from the goat, he immediately freed the goat and started to engage in reciting the ninth chapter of the *Srimad Bhagavad-gita* daily and thus he also gained the lotus feet of Lord Govinda.

The Glories of Chapter Ten

Lord Siva said: My dear Parvati, I will now relate to you the glories of the tenth chapter of the *Srimad Bhagavad-gita,* which are themselves a stairway to the spiritual world.

In Kashipuri, there was a *brahmana* of the name Dhirabuddhi, who was as dear to me as Nandi, my carrier. He was always peaceful and all his senses were fixed in the glorification of Lord Krishna. Wherever he would go, I would follow him with great love, so that I could protect and serve him. Seeing my activities, my eternal servant Bhringiriddhi inquired from me: What kind of austerities and other pious activities has this great devotee performed, that you are personally rendering service to him?

Hearing Bhringiriddhi's inquiry I replied: Once, in Kailash Parvata, in the garden known as *punnaag,* I was enjoying sitting in the moonlight, and suddenly there was a great wind, which caused the trees to shake with a loud noise. A shadow was cast all around as if a mountain was moving. In the sky, a large bird, the color of a rain cloud, appeared. Due to the flapping of its wings, it was causing the trees to shake and the dust to swirl around. The bird landed on the ground and offered his respects and also a beautiful lotus flower to me. After which, he said, "O Mahadeva! All glories to you, the shelter of all. There is no limit to your glories. You are the protector of the devotees who have control over their senses. And you are the foremost of all the devotees of the Supreme Lord Krishna. Great souls such as Brihaspati are always chanting your glories. But even the thousand-headed Ananta Sesa, is not able to fully describe your glories. So what to speak of a bird like me, having such small intelligence."

After hearing the bird's prayer, I inquired, "Who are you, and where are you coming from? You look like a swan and your bodily color is that of a crow." The bird said, "Please understand that I am the swan carrier of Lord Brahma. And the reason for my body having attained a black color, I will relate to you.

"Just close to Saurashtra (Surat) there is a beautiful lake, from where this wonderful heavenly lotus came. I had been enjoying there for some time. Just as I was flying away, I suddenly fell to the ground and my body took on this black color. At that time I was thinking to myself, 'How have I fallen down, and how has my body which was white like camphor turned black?' While thinking in this way I heard a voice, coming from the lotuses in the lake, 'O swan, get up, I will tell you the reason why you fell down, and your body turned black.' I got up and went to the center of the lake. There I saw five extraordinary beautiful lotuses, out of which came a very beautiful lady. After circumambulating her, I asked the reason for my falling down. She replied, 'O black swan, while you were flying, you flew over me, and due to this offense, your body has now become black. When I saw you fall down, I felt sorry for you, and thus, I called you here. When I opened my mouth, the scent emanating from it purified seven thousand black bees, who immediately attained admission into the heavenly realm. My dear king of birds, the reason I have such power I will tell you.

"'Previous to this birth, three births before, I was born in a *brahmana* family, and my name was Sarojavadana. My father had always instructed me in the principles of chastity and when I got married I served my husband very faithfully. One day I found a maina (a black bird), and due to looking after it, my service to my husband became affected. He became angry, and cursed me to become a maina in my next birth.

"'In my next birth I became a maina, but due to my following the principles of chastity strictly, I managed to come in contact with some sages, who kept me at their ashram. A daughter of one of the sages looked after me. While staying there, every morning and evening, I would hear the recitation of the tenth chapter of the *Srimad Bhagavad-gita*. Due to which, in my next birth, I attained the body of an apsara named Padmavati and resided in the heavenly planets. One day, I was traveling in a flower airplane when I saw the beautiful lotus flower on this lake. Coming here, I started to enjoy in the water. At that time, Durvasa Muni arrived and saw me completely naked. Being afraid of him I immediately took the form of five lotuses. My two arms became two lotuses and my two legs became two lotuses, and the rest of my body became the fifth lotus. From Durvasa Muni's eyes fire started to emanate. He said that I was sinful and would stay in that form for one hundred years. After cursing me, he immediately disappeared. But fortunately, I was able to remember the tenth chapter of the *Srimad Bhagavad-gita*. And today, I have become free from the curse. Due to your crossing over me, you fell to the ground and your body became black, but if you hear from me the tenth chapter of the *Srimad Bhagavad-gita,* you will become free from this situation.'

"After Padmavati had completed reciting the tenth chapter of the *Srimad Bhagavad-gita,* she left in an airplane for Vaikuntha. After that I came here and offered this beautiful lotus from that lake to you."

Lord Siva said: After the black swan completed his story he immediately gave up his body and took birth in a *brahmana* family as Dhirabuddhi, who, from his childhood, always chanted the tenth chapter of the *Srimad Bhagavad-gita*.

Whoever heard that chanting, whether they were fallen and addicted to intoxication, or even killers of *brahmana*s, would attain the *darshan* of Lord Vishnu, who is holding the Shankha and Chakra. For that reason my dear Bhringiriddhi, I am always serving Dhirabuddhi.

My dear Parvati, whether one be male, female, sannyasi, or grhastha, in fact, whatever situation one may be in, if he chants the tenth chapter of the *Srimad Bhagavad-gita,* he will attain the *darshan* of Lord Vishnu.

The Glories of Chapter Eleven

Lord Siva said: My dear Parvati, now I will relate to you the glories of the eleventh chapter of the *Srimad Bhagavad-gita*. It is not possible to tell it's full glories as there are thousands of stories. I will relate one of them only.

On the banks of the Pranita river is the large town Megankara where the famous temple of Jagat Isvara is situated. Jagat Isvara is holding a bow in His hand. In Megankara, there was a pure *brahmana* of the name Sunand, who remained a *brahmachari* his whole life.

Sunand would sit in front of Lord Jagat Isvara and recite the eleventh chapter of the *Srimad Bhagavad-gita* and remember the Universal Form of the Lord. By reciting the eleventh chapter of the *Srimad Bhagavad-gita,* he gained complete control over his senses and was able to remember Lord Jagat Isvara continuously.

Once that pure *brahmana* Sunand went on a tour of the holy places on the banks of the Godavari River. He visited all the sacred places, starting with Viraj-Tirtha. In all these holy places he took bath and *darshan* of the presiding deity. One day he reached the town of Vivaha Mandap. Along with his associates he searched for a place to stay and eventually in the middle of the town they found a *dharmashala*, where they took rest for the night. When Sunand woke up in the morning he found that all his associates had left. While searching for them, he met the headman of the town, who immediately fell at his feet and said, "O great sage, I cannot say where your associates have gone, but I can tell you that there is no devotee equal to you. I have never seen anyone as pure as you. Oh, my dear *brahmana*, I am begging you to stay in this town."

When Sunand heard the humble request of the headman of the town, he decided to stay for some days. The headman made every arrangement for the comfortable stay of Sunand and engaged in his service day and night. After eight days had passed, a villager came before Sunand. Crying very loudly, he said, "O pure *brahmana*, last night a rakshasa ate my son." Sunand asked, "Where does that rakshasa stay? And how did he eat your son?"

The villager replied, "In this town a very frightful *rakshasa* lives. Everyday he used to eat the villagers whenever he pleased. One day, we all went to the *rakshasa* and requested him to protect us, and in return we would provide him with his daily food. The *dharmashala* was built, and any travelers who came here were sent there to stay and while they were sleeping the rakshasa would eat them. In this way we have been able to protect ourselves from the *rakshasa*. You, along with your associates, stayed at the *dharmashala*, but the *rakshasa* did not eat you along with everyone else. I will tell you the reason.

"Last night a friend of my son came but I did not realize that he was a close and dear friend of my son, so I sent him to stay in the *dharmashala*. Later when my son found out, he went after him to try and bring him back. When he went there, he was also eaten by the *rakshasa*. Today, in the morning, I went to the *rakshasa* and asked him, why he had eaten my son along with the other travelers. I also asked him if there was any way I could get my son back.

"The *rakshasa* told me, 'I did not know that your son had also entered the *dharmashala*, thus he was eaten with everyone else. As far as getting him back, that will be possible when I am freed from this *rakshasa* body, by the mercy of a person who recites the eleventh chapter of the *Srimad Bhagavad-gita* daily. Right now, there is a *brahmana* staying in this town, who had stayed at the *dharmashala*, but I had not eaten him, because he daily recites the eleventh chapter of the *Srimad Bhagavad-gita.* If he recites the eleventh chapter seven times and sprinkles water on me, then I will get free from the curse of this *rakshasa* body.'"

Sunand asked the villager, "What sin did this person perform to attain a *rakshasa* body?"

The villager replied, "Long ago there had been a farmer living here. One day he was guarding the fields when, just a little distance away from him, a large vulture attacked a person, who was traveling on the road. At that time, a yogi was passing by and when he saw the person being attacked he came running to his aid but he was too late. Then the yogi became angry with the farmer and spoke to him as follows, 'One who sees others in danger from thieves, snakes, fire, attack by weapons and so forth, and even though he is capable of helping them, he does not come to help, is punished by Yamaraja. After suffering in hell for a very long time, he takes birth as a wolf. And one, who helps someone in need of help, certainly pleases Lord Vishnu. One, who attempts to save a cow from the hands of a ferocious animal, a low-class man, or a wicked ruler, attains Lord Vishnu. Wicked farmer, you saw the vulture attacking that person but still you made no attempt to save him. Now I curse you to take birth as a rakshasa.' The farmer said, 'I was watching the fields for the whole night and I am very tired, so kindly be merciful to me, O gentle sage.' The yogi replied, 'When someone, who is daily reciting the eleventh chapter of the *Srimad Bhagavad-gita,* sprinkles water on your head, then you will become free from this curse.'"

The villager said, "My dear Sunand, with your hand kindly sprinkle water on the head of this *rakshasa*." After hearing this history from the villager, Sunand went with him to the place where the *rakshasa* was staying and while reciting the eleventh chapter of the *Srimad Bhagavad-gita,* he sprinkled water on the *rakshasa's* head. The *rakshasa* immediately attained a four-armed form like that of Lord Vishnu. Not only he, but all the thousands of persons he had eaten also attained a four-armed form like that of Lord Vishnu. Then they all sat down in the flower aeroplane, which had been sent to take them to Vaikuntha.

Seeing those amazing events, the villager inquired which one was his son. The person who had been the *rakshasa* started to laugh and indicated towards one of those thousands of beautiful persons sitting in the transcendental airplane. He replied, "He is your son." The villager requested his son to come home with him. Hearing his father's request the son smilingly replied, "My dear sir, many times you have been my son and I yours, but now by the grace of this great pure devotee Sunand, I have been released from the wheel of birth and death and now I am going to my real home, Vaikuntha. Dear sir, kindly surrender unto the lotus feet of Sunand and hear from him the eleventh chapter of the *Srimad Bhagavad-gita,* and you will also attain the abode of Lord Vishnu (Vaikuntha). Of this there is no doubt. From Lord Krishna's mouth, these nectarean instructions came on the battlefield of Kuruksetra in reply to the questions of His friend Arjuna. By hearing and reciting this discourse, one can break the tight knot which is binding us to the wheel of birth and death."

Lord Siva said: After speaking those words, full of wisdom, he went to Vaikuntha with all those other fortunate souls. And his father learned the eleventh chapter of the *Srimad Bhagavad-gita* from Sunand and very soon they also went to Vaikuntha.

My dear Parvati, you have heard the glories of the eleventh chapter of the *Srimad Bhagavad-gita,* which is capable of destroying all sinful reactions.

The Glories of Chapter Twelve

Lord Siva said: I will recite the wonderful glories of the twelfth chapter of the *Srimad Bhagavad-gita* before you, dear Parvati.

In the South there is an important holy place by the name of Kolbapur, where the temple of the Lord's divine consort Maha Lakshmi is situated. Maha Lakshmi is continually worshipped by all the demigods. That place is the fulfiller of all desires and Rudragaya is also situated there. One day, a young prince arrived there. His body was the color of gold. His eyes were very beautiful. His shoulders were very strong and his chest was broad. His arms were long and strong. When he arrived in Kolbapur, he first went to the lake known as Manikanth-tirth, where he took bath and offered worship to his ancestors. Then he went to the temple of Maha Lakshmi, where he offered obeisances, and prayed, "O Devi, whose heart is full of mercy, who is worshipped throughout the three worlds and who is the giver of all fortune and the Mother of Creation. All glories to you, O shelter of all living entities, O fulfiller of all desires, you are the wonderful energy of Lord Achyuta, who is maintaining the three worlds. You are the supreme goddess. O protector of the devotees, all glories to you. O Devi, it is you who fulfills the desires of the devotees, and it is you, who engages them in the service of Lord Achyuta. You are eternal and the deliverer of all fallen souls. All glories unto you. O Devi, for the welfare and protection of the three worlds, you take on many forms such as Ambika, Brahmi, Vaishnavi, Maheshwari, Varahi Maha-Lakshmi, Narasimhi, Indri, Kumari, Chandika, Lakshmi, Savitri, Chandrakala, Rohini, Parameshwari. All glories unto you, whose glories are unlimited. Kindly be merciful to me."

When Maha Lakshmi heard those prayers, She became very pleased and said to the prince, "O prince, I am very happy with you, please request any benediction from me according to your heart's desire."

The prince said, "O mother of the three worlds, my father, King Brahadratha was performing the famous sacrifice known as Ashwamedha. But before completing the yajna, he died due to disease. And before I was able to complete the Ashwamedha yajna, someone stole the horse that had traveled all over the world and had been purified for sacrifice. I sent persons in all directions in search of the horse, but they were unable to find it. Then I took permission from the priest to come and pray for your help. And, if you are pleased with me, then kindly let me know, how I can get back the horse and complete the fire sacrifice and thus fulfill my father's desire."

Maha Lakshmi said, "Oh noble prince, by the gate of my temple lives a highly elevated *brahmana*, who is known by the name Siddha-Samadhi. He can fulfill your desire."

When the prince heard these words of Maha Lakshmi, he went to the place where Siddha-Samadhi lived and offered obeisances to him. After having offered obeisances, he stood before Siddha-Samadhi silently with folded hands. Siddha-Samadhi then said, "You have been sent here by mother Maha Lakshmi, so I will fulfill your desire."

Then chanting some mantras, Siddha-Samadhi brought all the demigods before him. The prince saw that all the demigods were standing before Siddha-Samadhi, awaiting his instructions. Siddha-Samadhi said to those demigods, "Oh devas, this prince's horse, which he had kept ready for sacrifice, was stolen at night by Lord Indra. Kindly bring that horse back now."

Immediately the demigods brought that horse before him, and Siddha-Samadhi dismissed them. When the prince saw these wonderful happenings, he fell at the feet of Siddha-Samadhi, and asked him, "How have you attained such power, which I have not seen or heard of anyone else possessing? O great sage, kindly hear my request. My father, King

Brahadratha, while beginning the Ashwamedha sacrifice, died unexpectedly. And I kept his body in pure boiled oil. Kindly, if you desire, bring him back to life."

Hearing this, Siddha-Samadhi gave a little chuckle, and said, "Let us go to the place, where you have kept your father's body." When they reached that place, Siddha-Samadhi took some water in his hand and while chanting mantras, he sprinkled water on the head of the dead body of King Brahadratha. As soon as the water touched his head, the king sat up and inquired from Siddha-Samadhi, "O great devotee, who are you?"

The prince immediately informed his father of all the events, which had taken place. When the king heard the narration, he again and again offered his obeisances to Siddha-Samadhi, and asked him, "What austerities have you performed to attain such divine powers?" Siddha-Samadhi replied, "My dear King Brahadratha, daily I recite the twelfth chapter of the *Srimad Bhagavad-gita*."

Hearing these words from that great devotee, the king learnt the twelfth chapter of the *Srimad Bhagavad-gita* from Siddha-Samadhi. In the course of time, both the king and his son attained the lotus feet of Lord Krishna. Many other persons have achieved the topmost goal, devotion to Lord Krishna's lotus feet, by daily reciting the twelfth chapter of the *Srimad Bhagavad-gita*.

The Glories of Chapter Thirteen

Lord Siva said: O Parvati, please hear the unlimited glories of the thirteenth chapter of the *Srimad Bhagavad-gita.* By hearing which you will become very happy.

In the South, there was a large river, Tungabhadra. On the banks of which there is a beautiful town of the name Hariharpur. There, the deity of Lord Siva, known by name Harihar, is worshiped. One who has his darshan attains auspicious things.

In Hariharpur lived a *brahmana* by the name of Hari-diksit, who was very learned, and lived a simple, austere life. His wife was called Durachara by the people because of her low-class activities. She would always speak to her husband in abusive language, and she had never slept with him. She was always rude to her husband's friends, and she would keep company with other men to satisfy her lusty desires. She was also addicted to various kinds of intoxicants. Seeing that the town was becoming more and more populated, she constructed a small structure in the forest where she could meet her lovers.

One night, feeling very lusty and not finding any lover to satisfy her, she went out to the forest to her meeting place, to see if any of her lovers were there. Not finding anyone at that place, and burning up with lust, she started to wander in the forest in the hope of finding someone to satisfy her. After having wandered for some time, and finding that her body, senses, and mind were paining so much, due to not being able to satisfy their lust, she became bewildered and sat down and started to cry.

Hearing the sound of her crying, a hungry tiger, who was sleeping, woke up and reached the place very quickly. Hearing the tiger coming, the lusty woman got up and thinking to herself that surely someone is coming who would satisfy her needs. She saw the tiger arrive in front of her. He was about to rip her apart with his sharp claws.

At that time, the lusty woman said, "O tiger, why have you come here to kill me? First you must tell me this and then you can kill me." The king of animals refrained from killing Durachara, and laughed. Then he related the following story.

"In the South there is a river of the name Malapaha. On the bank of which is the town of Muniparna. At that place is a famous deity of Lord Siva, known as Panchalinga. In that town I had taken birth in a *brahmana* family. Although I had taken such a high birth, I was still very greedy, and had no control over my senses. I used to sit on the banks of the river and perform sacrifices for persons who were not qualified to partake in such performances. I would also eat from the homes of materialistic persons. I would collect more funds than necessary in the name of performing sacrifices and worship of the deity, and use the same for my own sense gratification. I would also criticize *brahmanas* who were strictly following the regulative principles, and I would never give charity to anyone. Slowly I became old, my hair turned white, my teeth fell out, my eyes became weak, but even still, I did not lose my lust to collect and hoard more funds. One day, by mistake, I went to beg some food at the house of some *brahmanas* who were very cruel and expert at cheating. They set the dogs on me. One of those dogs bit my leg and I fell over and very quickly died. After that, I attained this tiger's body, and I am living in this dangerous forest.

"Fortunately, I am able to remember my last birth and in this birth I do not attack any devotee, sannyasi, or chaste lady. I take only sinful persons and unchaste women as my food. As you are the most unchaste and sinful woman, you will definitely become my lunch."

When the tiger finished his narration, he devoured the sinful woman. Thereafter, the Yamadutas threw her into the hell known as Duyada, which is a lake full of stool, urine, and blood. She had to stay in that filthy place for ten million *kalpas*. Then she was thrown into the hell known as Raurava, where she stayed for one hundred *manvantaras.* Then she took birth on earth as a female *chandala,* and again she lived in the same sinful way. Due to her sinful activities, she got leprosy and tuberculosis. By chance and good fortune, she once went to the holy place of Hariharpur. Close to the temple of Jambakadevi (Parvati), she saw the great saint Vasudeva who was always reciting the thirteenth chapter of the *Srimad Bhagavad-gita*. From his mouth she heard the recitation, and becoming attracted, she heard it again and again. By that hearing, she gave up the body of a *chandala* and became completely free from the reactions of her past sinful activities. She attained a four-armed form similar to Lord Vishnu, and was taken to Vaikuntha.

The Glories of Chapter Fourteen

Lord Siva said: O Parvati kindly hear from me the glories of the fourteenth chapter of the *Srimad Bhagavad-gita*, with the greatest attention.

In Simhaldvip was a king of the name Vikram-Betal. One day, he went to the forest to go hunting with his son and two hunting dogs. When he reached the forest he released one dog to chase a rabbit. When the dog was chasing it, the rabbit looked as if it was flying. Running and running, the rabbit reached a beautiful hermitage, which was very peaceful. The deer were sitting happily under the shade of the trees. The monkeys were joyfully eating the fruits of those trees. The tiger cubs were playing with the baby elephants, and the snakes were crawling over the peacocks.

In this forest lived the great sage Vatsa, who worshipped Lord Krishna by reciting the fourteenth chapter of the *Srimad Bhagavad-gita.* Near the ashram of Maharaja Vatsa, one of his disciples was washing his feet while chanting the fourteenth chapter of the *Srimad Bhagavad-gita*. The earth at that spot became wet. Just then the rabbit came running and slipped in the mud. Immediately the rabbit attained a heavenly body. An airplane came down, picked him up, and took him off to the heavenly planets. After a moment, the dog arrived there in search of the rabbit, and he also slipped in the mud. He gave up that dog body, attained a heavenly body, and was also taken off to the heavenly planets.

Seeing all of this, the disciple of Maharaja Vatsa started to laugh. King Vikram-Betal, having witnessed these amusing events asked the *brahmana*, "How is it possible that the rabbit and dog went off to heaven in front of our eyes?" The *brahmana* said, "In this forest, the great sage Vatsa, who has completely conquered his senses, is always engaged in chanting the fourteenth chapter of the *Srimad Bhagavad-gita*. I am his disciple, and I am also, by his grace, always engaged in chanting the fourteenth chapter of the *Srimad Bhagavad-gita*. Due to the rabbit and dog slipping in the mud, which had been made wet from the water that had washed my feet, they both attained the higher planets.

Now I will tell you the reason why I was laughing. In Maharastra is the town Pratudhak. A *brahmana* called Keshava had lived there. He was the most cruel of men. His wife's name was Vilobana. She was a very loose lady, who always enjoyed the company of other men. For this reason, her husband became angry and killed her. In her next life she became the dog. And the *brahmana* Keshava, due to his sinful activities, became the rabbit."

Lord Siva said: After hearing the glories of the fourteenth chapter of the *Srimad Bhagavad-gita,* King Vikram-Betal also began daily reciting the fourteenth chapter of the *Srimad Bhagavad-gita.* When he gave up his body, he went to Vaikuntha where he engaged eternally in the service of the lotus feet of Lord Vishnu.

The Glories of Chapter Fifteen

Lord Siva said: My dear Parvati, now I will tell you the glories of the Fifteenth Chapter of the *Srimad Bhagavad-gita.* Kindly listen carefully.

In Gaudadesa, there was a king of the name Narasingha. He was so powerful that he was able to defeat the demigods. The commander of his army, Sarabhmerund, was greedy and along with the prince, planned to kill the king, and become the ruler of Gaudadesa. But before he could carry out his plan, he got cholera and died very quickly. He took his next birth as a horse in the country known as Sindhu. The horse was beautiful and a fast runner. He had all the qualities of a prize horse. One day, the son of a rich man of Gaudadesa saw the horse and decided to buy him with the intention of selling him to the king of Gaudadesa. He purchased the horse and took him to the capital of Gaudadesa. When he reached the city he went straight to the palace of the king and requested the guards to inform the king of his arrival.

He came before the king who asked him, "What has brought you here?" That businessman replied, "O king, in Sindhu I found a horse of the highest quality and it's equal cannot be found in the whole universe. I paid a large sum of money for it." The king ordered, "Bring the horse immediately." The horse was brought before the king who became very pleased with the high qualities of the horse. After examining the horse, the king paid the businessman whatever amount he had requested without thinking twice.

Some days later, the king decided to go hunting. Riding that horse, he went to the forest, where he saw a deer, and immediately he gave chase. He followed the deer in every direction it turned. After some time the rest of his party got left far behind. After chasing for a long time and becoming tired and thirsty, he stopped to take rest. He tied the horse to the branch of a tree and he sat down on a large rock.

After a little while he saw a piece of parchment blowing in the wind and it landed next to him on the rock. On the piece of parchment was written half a sloka of the fifteenth chapter of the *Srimad Bhagavad-gita*. The king started to read out loud, and as the first sound came out of his mouth, the horse fell down to the ground and gave up that horse body. He attained a transcendental four-armed form and immediately sat down in a flower airplane, which had come to take him to that transcendental abode Vaikuntha.

The king noticed that close by, there was a beautiful ashram, which was surrounded by fruit trees. Sitting in the ashram was a *brahmana* who had complete control over his senses. The king went there and offered respects to the *brahmana.* With folded hands, the king asked, "How was it possible that my horse attained Vaikuntha?" The *brahmana*, whose name was Vishnusharma, replied, "O king, previously, you had a commander-in-chief of your army, who was known by the name Sarabhmerund. He had planned along with the prince to usurp you from your throne. Before he was able to do so, he got cholera and died. After which he took birth as that horse. By chance, he heard some words from the fifteenth chapter of the *Srimad Bhagavad-gita* and attained Vaikuntha."

The king offered his respects to the *brahmana* and returned to his capital. Again and again he read what was written on the parchment. After a short time he installed his son as the king of Gaudadesa and he went off to the forest, where he regularly recited the fifteenth chapter of the *Srimad Bhagavad-gita* and quickly attained the lotus feet of Lord Vishnu.

The Glories of Chapter Sixteen

Lord Siva said: My dear Parvati, I will now tell you the glories of the sixteenth chapter of the *Srimad Bhagavad-gita*.

In Gujarat, in the town called Sourastra (Surat), King Khadgabahu had his kingdom and he lived there just like another Indra, the king of heaven. He kept a passionate male elephant, Arimardana, from whose temples liquid oozed due to his pride. One day the elephant, in a fit of anger, broke loose from his chains and started to destroy the elephant shed. Then he ran here and there, wildly chasing the citizens. Everyone fled as fast as possible. The elephant keepers immediately reported the news to the king. The king went to see the elephant, along with his son. King Khadgabahu knew the art of controlling wild elephants. When the king reached the place where the elephant was running amok, he saw that many persons had been trampled and others were running here and there trying to get away from the elephant.

Just then, as the king was watching the chaotic scene, he saw a *brahmana* peacefully returning from taking his bath in the lake. The *brahmana* was silently reciting the first three *slokas* from the sixteenth chapter of the *Srimad Bhagavad-gita,* which start with the word *abhayam,* fearlessness. The people tried to tell the *brahmana* not to go near elephant, but he did not take any notice of them. He walked straight up to the mad elephant and started to stroke him. When the elephant saw the *brahmana* approaching, he lost all anger and lay down peacefully.

The *brahmana* patted the elephant for a few moments, and then he went peacefully on his way. When the king and the citizens saw this amazing incident, they were astonished. The king went and fell at the feet of the *brahmana* and asked him, "What austerities and worship have you performed to attain such peacefulness and amazing powers?" The *brahmana* replied, "Daily I am reciting some *slokas* from the sixteenth chapter of the *Srimad Bhagavad-gita*."

Lord Siva said: The king requested the *brahmana* to come to his palace. There he offered one hundred gold coins to him in charity, and requested that pious *brahmana* to instruct him in the chanting of those verses from the sixteenth chapter of the *Srimad Bhagavad-gita.*

King Khadgabahu chanted those verses for some time. One day he went with his guards to the place where the elephant was kept and ordered the elephant keepers to release him. The citizens became upset with the king thinking that the elephant would run amok again. The king went before the elephant. It immediately lay down and the king started to stroke it. After that the king returned to his palace and installed his son on the throne. He left for the forest, where he worshiped Lord Krishna by chanting those *slokas* from the sixteenth chapter of the *Srimad Bhagavad-gita* and quickly he attained the lotus feet of Lord Krishna.

Anyone who chants the sixteenth chapter of the *Srimad Bhagavad-gita,* however sinful he is, very quickly attains the same goal as King Khadgabahu—the lotus feet of Lord Krishna.

The Glories of Chapter Seventeen

Lord Siva said: My dear Parvati, you have heard the unlimited glories of the sixteenth chapter of the *Srimad Bhagavad-gita*. Now, kindly hear the nectarean glories of the seventeenth chapter of the *Srimad Bhagavad-gita*.

King Khadgabahu's son had a crafty and exceptionally foolish servant called Dushasan. Dushasan made a bet with the prince that he could ride the elephant. He jumped upon the elephant and after going a few steps, the people there requested him not to ride that dangerous elephant. But foolish Dushasan started to prod the elephant and used strong words to urge him on. Suddenly, the elephant became very angry and started to run wildly here and there. Unable to hold on, Dushasan fell to the ground. The elephant stomped on him and Dushasan died. He attained the body of an elephant in Simbaldwip, where he stayed in the king's palace.

The king of Simbaldwip was a close friend of King Khadgabahu. One day the king of Simhaldwip decided to send the elephant as a present to his friend, King Khadgabahu. He, in turn, presented it to a poet, who pleased him with his beautiful poetry.

Thereafter, the poet sold the elephant for one hundred gold coins to the king of Malva. After some time, the elephant contracted a terminal disease. When the elephant keepers saw that the elephant had stopped eating and drinking, they reported the matter to the king. The king went to see the elephant, along with the best doctors. At that time, to the surprise of the king, the elephant started to speak. It said, "My dear king you are very pious, and a strict follower of the *Vedas*. You always worship the lotus feet of Lord Vishnu. So you should know that at this time, these medicines and doctors will be of no use. Neither any kind of charity or sacrifice will help at the time of death. If you care for me and want to help me, then bring someone who daily recites the seventeenth chapter of the *Srimad Bhagavad-gita*."

As requested by the elephant, the king brought a great devotee, who regularly recited the seventeenth chapter of the *Srimad Bhagavad-gita.* The devotee, while chanting the seventeenth chapter, sprinkled water on the elephant. The elephant gave up his body and attained a four-armed form similar to that of Lord Vishnu. He sat down in a flower airplane, which had been sent to take him to Vaikuntha. While sitting in the airplane, the king inquired from him about his previous birth. Dushasan explained everything to the king and then he left for Vaikuntha. After which, the best of men, the king of Malva, started regularly reciting the seventeenth chapter of the *Srimad Bhagavad-gita*. After a short time he attained the lotus feet of Lord Krishna.

THE GLORIES OF CHAPTER EIGHTEEN

Parvati said: My dear husband, you have told me the glories of the seventeenth chapter of the *Srimad Bhagavad-gita*. Now kindly relate the glories of the eighteenth chapter of the *Srimad Bhagavad-gita*.

Lord Siva said: Oh daughter of the Himalayas [Parvati], please listen to the glories of the eighteenth chapter of the *Srimad Bhagavad-gita,* which is higher than the *Vedas* and the giver of unlimited bliss. When it enters into one's ears it destroys all material desires. For the pure devotee, it is divine nectar, it is Lord Vishnu's very life, and it is a solace to the hearts of Lord Indra and the demigods, as well as the great yogis headed by Sanak and Sananda.

One who recites it sends the messengers of Yamaraja far away. There is no other recitation, which can so quickly destroy all sin and free one from the threefold miseries of this world. Now listen with great devotion.

On the topmost peak of Mount Meru is Amaravati, which was built by Vishvakarma. In that heavenly kingdom, Lord Indra and his wife Saci are served by the demigods. One day while Lord Indra was sitting peacefully, he saw that a beautiful person had arrived there, whom the servants of Lord Vishnu were serving. When Lord Indra saw the beautiful young person, he immediately fell from his throne to the ground. At that time the demigods, who had been worshipping Indra, picked up Indra's crown and placed it on the head of the beautiful person. Then all the demigods and other denizens of the heavenly planets started to perform aratik and sing wonderful songs to the new King Indra. The great *rishis* came there and offered their blessings and chanted Vedic mantras, and the Gandharvas and Apsaras started to sing and dance joyfully. In this way, the new Indra, who had not performed the usual one hundred horse sacrifices, started to enjoy hundreds of different types of services rendered by the demigods and other denizens of the heavenly planets. When the old Indra saw this he became very surprised.

He thought to himself, "This person here has never built wells or dug *kunds* or planted trees for the welfare of others, and when there were droughts, he did not provide grains in charity. He never performed any fire sacrifices or great charities in the holy places. How has he managed to attain my seat?" The old Indra, feeling greatly disturbed in his mind, went to the ocean of milk to pray to Lord Vishnu. When he obtained the *darshan* of Lord Vishnu, he asked Him, "My dear Lord Vishnu, in the past I performed many sacrifices and other pious activities, for which I was installed as the lord of heaven. But now another person has come and taken my place as the king of heaven. This person in his life never performed any great, wonderful pious activities, nor had he performed any great Vedic sacrifices. How is it possible that he has obtained my throne?"

Lord Vishnu said, "My dear Indra, that great soul has daily performed the recitation of the eighteenth chapter of the *Srimad Bhagavad-gita*. Everyday during his life, he recited five *slokas* from this chapter, and because of that activity he has attained the results of all sorts of pious activities and *yajnas* and after enjoying for many years as the king of heaven, he will attain My personal abode. If you perform the same activity of reciting the eighteenth chapter of the *Srimad Bhagavad-gita,* you can also attain My divine abode."

After hearing Lord Vishnu's words, Lord Indra took the form of a *brahmana* and went to the bank of the Godavari River, where he saw the town of Kalegrani, which is very sacred. At that place, the Supreme Lord in His form known as Kalesva, resides. Close to this town, on the bank of the Godavari river, a pure *brahmana* was sitting, who was very merciful and had understood the topmost goal and secret of the Vedic literatures. Daily he would sit at that spot and recite the *slokas* of the eighteenth chapter of the *Srimad Bhagavad-gita*. When Lord Indra saw him he became very happy. He immediately fell at his lotus feet and requested him to teach him the eighteenth chapter of the *Srimad Bhagavad-gita*. Lord Indra then practiced the recitation of the eighteenth chapter of the *Srimad Bhagavad-gita* for sometime and he attained the topmost place of Vishnuloka. When he attained that place, he realized that the pleasure he had enjoyed as King Indra, along with the demigods, was nothing in comparison.

My dear Parvati, for this reason the great sages especially chant the eighteenth chapter of the *Srimad Bhagavad-gita* and by so doing very quickly attain the lotus feet of Lord Vishnu.

Anyone who hears or studies this *Gita Mahatmya* very quickly destroys all sins, which he has accumulated. And that person, who remembers this discourse with great faith attains the results of all kinds of pious activities and great sacrifices, and after enjoying all worldly opulences, attains the abode of Lord Vishnu.

Thus ends the glories of the *Srimad Bhagavad-gita* as spoken by Lord Siva to his wife Parvati Devi.

Index of Slokas& Their Speakers

Chapter	Dhritarastra	Sanjaya	Arjuna	Lord Krishna	Total Slokas
1	1	25	20	0	46
2	0	3	6	63	72
3	0	0	3	40	43
4	0	0	1	41	42
5	0	0	1	28	29
6	0	0	5	42	47
7	0	0	0	30	30
8	0	0	2	26	28
9	0	0	0	34	34
10	0	0	7	35	42
11	0	0	33	14	55
12	0	0	1	19	20
13	0	0	1	34	35
14	0	0	1	26	27
15	0	0	0	20	20
16	0	0	0	24	24
17	0	0	1	27	28
18	0	5	2	71	78
Total	1	41	84	574	700

Gītā Māhātmyam by Śrī Śankarācarya

1

gītā-śāstram idaṁ puṇyaṁ, yaḥ paṭhet prayataḥ pumān
viṣṇoḥ padam avāpnoti, bhaya-śokādi-varjitaḥ.

One who recites the *Bhagavad-gītā* scripture, which is the bestower of all virtue, with devotion and a regulated mind, will attain to a holy abode such as Vaikuntha, the residence of Lord Viṣṇu. That place is always free from the mundane qualities based on fear and lamentation.

2

gītādhyāyana-śīlasya, prāṇāyama-parasya ca
naiva santi hi pāpāni, pūrva-janma-kṛtāni ca

If one reads *Bhagavad-gītā* very sincerely and with all seriousness, then by the grace of the Lord the reactions of his past misdeeds will not act upon him.

3

maline mocanaṁ puṁsāṁ, jala-snānaṁ dine dine
sakṛd gītāmṛta-snānaṁ, saṁsāra-mala-nāśanam

One may cleanse himself daily by taking a bath in water, but if one takes a bath even once in the sacred Ganges water of *Bhagavad-gītā,* for him the dirt of material life is altogether vanquished.

4

gītā su-gītā kartavyā, kim anyaiḥ śāstra-vistaraiḥ
yā svayaṁ padmanābhasya, mukha-padmād viniḥsṛtā

Because *Bhagavad-gītā* is spoken by the Supreme Personality of Godhead, one need not read any other Vedic literature. One need only attentively and regularly hear and read *Bhagavad-gītā.* In the present age, people are so absorbed in mundane activities that it is not possible for them to read all the Vedic literatures, but this is not necessary. This one book, *Bhagavad-gītā,* will suffice, because it is the essence of all Vedic literatures and especially because it is spoken by the Supreme Personality of Godhead.

5

bhāratāmṛta-sarvasvaṁ, viṣṇu-vaktrād viniḥsṛtam
gītā-gaṅgodakaṁ pītvā, punar janma na vidyate

By drinking the Ganges waters of the *Gītā,* the divine quintessence of the *Mahābhārat* emanating from the holy lotus mouth of Lord Viṣṇu, one will never take rebirth in the material world again. In other words, by devotionally reciting the *Gītā,* the cycle of birth and death is terminated.

6

sarvopaniṣado gāvo, dogdhā gopāla-nandanaḥ pārtho
vatsaḥ su-dhīr bhoktā, dugdhaṁ gītāmṛtaṁ mahat

All the Upanisads are like a cow, and the milker of the cow is Sri Kṛṣṇa, the son of Nanda. Arjuna is the calf, the beautiful nectar of the *Gita* is the milk, and the fortunate devotees of fine theistic intellect are the drinkers and enjoyers of that milk.

7

ekaṁ śāstraṁ devakī-putra-gītam
eko devo devakī-putra eva
eko mantras tasya nāmāni yāni
karmāpy ekaṁ tasya devasya sevā

There need be only one holy scripture—the divine *Gītā* sung by Lord Śrī Kṛṣṇa: only one worshipable Lord—Lord Śrī Kṛṣṇa; only one mantra—His holy names; and only one duty—devotional service unto that Supreme Worshipable Lord, Śrī Kṛṣṇa.

Śrīmad-Bhāgavat Māhātmya

of

Skanda Purāṇa

"O Brahmā, O Suvrata, among all types of festivals, the festival of discussing *Śrīmad-Bhāgavatam* is the topmost. Those who participate in such festivals for My pleasure and hear *Śrīmad-Bhāgavatam* with devotion and those who worship *Śrīmad-Bhāgavatam* with cloth, ornaments, flowers, lamp, and incense certainly control Me just as a chaste wife controls her good husband."

INTRODUCTION

Śrīla Bhaktisiddhānta Sarasvatī Ṭhākura Prabhupāda used to say that if all the literatures and scriptures in this world are burnt to ashes, but only *Śrīmad-Bhāgavatam* remains, nothing is lost.

Śrīmad-Bhāgavatam is the last literary contribution of Srila Vyasadeva after his maturity of devotional practice. Thus *Śrīmad-Bhāgavatam* is extremely dear to the devotees of Lord Kṛṣṇa. It is relishable by the best of all *paramahamsa* devotees. It is therefore appropriately called *paramahamsa-saṁhitā*.

From *Garuḍa Purāṇa*, we find this statement about *Śrīmad-Bhāgavatam*:

artho 'yaṁ brahma-sūtrāṇāṁ bhāratārtha-vinirṇayaḥ
gāyatrī-bhāṣya-rūpo 'sau vedārtha-paribṛṁhitaḥ
purāṇānāṁ sāma-rūpaḥ sākṣād-bhagavatoditaḥ
dvādaśa-skandha-yukto 'yaṁ śata-viccheda-saṁyutaḥ
grantho 'ṣṭādaśa-sāhasraḥ śrīmad-bhāgavatābhidhaḥ

'The meaning of the Vedānta-sūtra is present in Śrīmad-Bhāgavatam. The full purport of the Mahābhārata is also there. The commentary of the Brahma-gāyatrī is also there and fully expanded with all Vedic knowledge. Śrīmad-Bhāgavatam is the supreme Purāṇa, and it was compiled by the Supreme Personality of Godhead in His incarnation as Vyāsadeva. There are twelve cantos, 335 chapters and eighteen thousand verses' (BBT translation)

sarva-vedetihāsānāṁ sāraṁ sāraṁ samuddhṛtam

The essence of all Vedic literature and all histories has been collected in Śrīmad-Bhāgavatam. (*Śrīmad-Bhāgavatam* 1.3.41)

sarva-vedānta-sāraṁ hi śrīmad-bhāgavatam iṣyate
tad-rasāmṛta-tṛptasya nānyatra syād ratiḥ kvacit

Śrīmad-Bhāgavatam is accepted as the essence of all Vedic literature and Vedānta philosophy. Whoever tastes the transcendental mellow of Śrīmad-Bhāgavatam is never attracted to any other literature. (*Śrīmad-Bhāgavatam* 12.13.15)

The glories of *Śrīmad-Bhāgavatam*, which devotees forever relish are unlimited. *Śrīmad-Bhāgavatam* is nondifferent from Lord Kṛṣṇa and attachment to it enables a *sādhaka* to have direct vision of the Lord. Lord Kṛṣṇa in the form of Lord Caitanya Mahāprabhu Himself declares:

kṛṣṇa-bhakti-rasa-svarūpa' śrī-bhāgavata
tāte veda-śāstra haite parama mahattva

Śrīmad-Bhāgavatam gives direct information of the mellow derived from service to Kṛṣṇa. Therefore Śrīmad-Bhāgavatam is above all other Vedic literatures. (*Caitanya-caritamṛta Madhya-līlā* 25:150)

Lord Śiva said about Śrīmad-Bhāgavatam:

ahaṁ vedmi śuko vetti vyāso vetti na vetti vā
bhaktyā bhāgavataṁ grāhyaṁ na buddhyā na ca ṭikayā

I know; Śukadeva Gosvāmī, the son of Vyāsadeva, know; and Vyāsadeva may know or may not know Śrīmad-Bhāgavatam. On the whole, Śrīmad-Bhāgavatam, the spotless Purāṇa, can be learned only through devotional service,

not by material intelligence, speculative methods or imaginary commentaries. (quoted in *Caitanya-caritamṛta Madhya-līlā* 24:313)

His Divine Grace A.C. Bhaktivedanta Swami Prabhupāda commented as follows on this verse: "Devotional service includes nine processes, beginning with hearing, chanting and remembering the activities of Lord Viṣṇu. Only one who has taken to devotional service can understand *Śrīmad-Bhāgavatam*, which is the spotless *Purāṇa* for a transcendentalist (*paramahaṁsa*). So-called commentaries are useless for this purpose. According to the Vedic injunction, *yasya deve parā bhaktir yathā deve tathā gurau* [*Śvetāśvatara Upaniṣad* 6.23]. All Vedic literatures maintain that Śrīmad-Bhāgavatam has to be learned from the person *bhāgavata*, and to understand it one has to engage in pure devotional service. *Śrīmad-Bhāgavatam* cannot be understood by so-called erudite scholars or grammarians. One who has developed pure Kṛṣṇa consciousness and has served the pure devotee, the spiritual master, can understand *Śrīmad-Bhāgavatam*. Others cannot."

A question may be raised on how is it that Lord Śiva and Sukadeva Gosvāmī know *Śrīmad-Bhāgavatam*, whereas Srila Vyasadeva, who is the author of the great book may or may not know *Śrīmad-Bhāgavatam*? The answer is that Lord Śiva first spoke *Śrīmad-Bhāgavatam* to Sukadeva Gosvāmī. Lord Śiva is the highest authority on *Kṛṣṇa bhakti*. The scriptures affirm *vaiṣṇavānāṁ yathā śambhuḥ*, among all the devotees of Lord Viṣṇu, Lord Śiva is the highest. Because Lord Śiva knows *Śrīmad-Bhāgavatam*, and because Sukadeva Gosvāmī heard *Śrīmad-Bhāgavatam* personally from Lord Śiva, Lord Śiva could therefore make this declaration.

Once, Pārvatīdevī, the wife of Lord Śiva, inquired from her husband about the garland of skulls which adorn his neck. She wanted to know from whose heads the skulls belong. Lord Śiva replied that these were her (Pārvatī's) heads. Surprised and curious, she asked how was that? Lord Śiva told her that because he loved her so much, each time she left her body, he took her head and put the skull on the garland around his neck. Satisfied, Pārvatī then told Lord Śiva that it seems she has had many lifetimes, but he had not. Lord Śiva said that was correct. She then inquired how he remains immortal. Lord Śiva replied that he is immortal because he is always absorbed in the nectarean narration of *Śrīmad-Bhāgavatam*. Desiring to also attain immortality, Pārvatīdevī asked Lord Śiva to narrate *Śrīmad-Bhāgavatam* to her. He agreed, under the condition that they select a private location, that there should be no other living entities present, and Pārvatīdevī must be very attentive and not fall asleep. Lord Śiva said the only way he could know she is listening was if she made a 'hum hum hum' sound', because the moment Lord Śiva starts speaking *Śrīmad-Bhāgavatam*, he enters *samadhi* and is unaware of externals.

A place was selected under a big mango tree, at a place known as Ekamravan, the present day Bhubaneswara, in Orissa India. Lord Śiva started speaking while Pārvatīdevī was responding 'hum hum hum'. Meanwhile Lord Śiva entered *samadhi* as a result of speaking *Śrīmad-Bhāgavatam*, but kept notice of the sound being vibrated by Pārvatīdevī. After a while Pārvatīdevī fell asleep, but the humming sound was still being vibrated. After sometime, Lord Śiva opened his eyes, and discovered that his wife was asleep, but he was still hearing this humming sound. Noticing the violation of the condition that no other living entity should hear him speaking *Śrīmad-Bhāgavatam*, Lord Śiva became angry and searched for the violator. He then looked on the branch of the tree and saw a parrot which was making the humming sound. Lord Śiva took his trident, desiring to kill the parrot. The parrot began to fly away while Lord Śiva chased after him. The parrot entered the ashram of Śrīla Vyāsadeva. At this time, Śrīla Vyāsadeva was engaged in reciting *Śrīmad-Bhāgavatam* to his wife. Her mouth was wide open as she listened to the *Śrīmad-Bhāgavatam* The parrot or Śuka immediately entered the wide-open mouth of the wife of Śrīla Vyāsadeva, and took shelter of her womb. Lord Śiva entered the ashram and inquired from the sage about the whereabouts of the parrot which he desired to kill. After hearing the cause of Lord Śiva's anger, Śrīla

Vyāsadeva calmed him by telling him that he could not kill the parrot, because it had attained immortality by hearing *Śrīmad-Bhāgavatam* directly from his mouth. Lord Śiva became satisfied and went back to his abode.

The lesson to be learned in this story is that the only auspicious path for anyone who wants to obtain relief from the scorching heat of material existence and obtain loving devotional service to Lord Kṛṣṇa, which is the only wealth of the devotees is by taking shelter of *Śrīmad-Bhāgavatam*.

I pray that this publication of *Śrīmad-Bhagavat-mahātmya* bring pleasure to the devotees, and thus I may be benefited.

Īṣvara dāsa
Completed on Nṛsiṁha Cāturdāsī 2001
Vṛndāvana-dhāma, India.

Chapter One

Śāṇḍilya Muni Describes Vrajabhū mi

Śrī Vyāsadeva said: In order to relish the mellows of devotional service, we continually offer our obeisances unto Lord Śrī Kṛṣṇa, whose eternal form is full of knowledge and bliss. He is supremely enchanting and the essence of all that is beautiful. He always showers unlimited happiness on the living entities by attracting them with the qualities of His beauty and sweetness. He is the cause of the creation, maintenance, and annihilation of innumerable universes.

The sages of Naimiṣāraṇya headed by Śaunaka, who are expert in relishing the nectarean topics of *Śrīmad-Bhāgavatam*, offered obeisances and asked the following question to Śrī Sūta Gosvāmī, who possesses all knowledge.

Śaunaka said: O best of the sages, after the great King Yudhiṣṭhira installed Śrī Vajranābha (the grandson of Pradyumna) at Mathurā, and Parīkṣit (his own grandson) at Hastināpura and then left to go back to Godhead, what did King Vajranābha and Mahārāja Parīkṣit do?

Śrīla Sūta Gosvāmī said: Before reciting this *Śrīmad-Bhāgavatam*, which is the very means of conquest, one should offer respectful obeisances unto the Personality of Godhead, Nārāyaṇa, unto Nara-nārāyaṇa Ṛṣi, the supermost human being, unto mother Sarasvatī, the goddess of learning, and unto Śrīla Vyāsadeva, the author.

O great sages headed by Śaunaka, after Yudhiṣṭhira went back to Godhead, Mahārāja Parīkṣit, desiring to see Vajranābha, went to Mathurā one day.

Vajranābha's heart was filled with affection when he heard that Mahārāja Parīkṣit, who was equal to his own father, was coming to see him. He went out of the city, fell at Mahārāja Parīkṣit's feet, and then brought him to his palace.

The great hero Mahārāja Parīkṣit, who was always absorbed in thoughts of Lord Kṛṣṇa, lovingly embraced Vajranābha. They entered the inner palace and offered obeisances to Rohiṇī, the chief of Lord Kṛṣṇa's one hundred and eight wives.

The wives welcomed the King according to custom. Mahārāja Parīkṣit then happily sat on a comfortable seat, and after resting a while he spoke to Vajranābha.

Mahārāja Parīkṣit said: Dear Vajranābha! Your father and grandfather saved my father and grandfather from great dangers. I was also fully protected by your great-grandfather, Lord Kṛṣṇa. Even if I wanted to repay their kindness, I would never be able to. Therefore I humbly request you to happily engage your subordinates in the affairs of the state. You should never worry about protecting your treasury, expanding your army, or subduing your enemies. Simply engage yourself in the service of your mothers.

Please tell me what is the cause of your distress and rest assured that I will dispel all your troubles.

Hearing Mahārāja Parīkṣit's words, Vajranābha was greatly pleased and he replied:

Mahārāja! Whatever you have told me is quite proper. Your father has greatly obliged me by instructing me in the science of archery. Therefore I have not even the slightest worry. By his mercy I have become expert in the military science of the *kṣatriyas*. I have only one problem. Please consider it.

Although I've been installed as the King of Mathurā, I feel like I am living in a secluded forest. The happiness of a kingdom is due to the people that live there, and I have no idea where the residents of this place have gone.

Hearing Vajranābha's words, Mahārāja Parīkṣit called for Śāṇḍilya Ṛṣi in order to clear Vajranābha's doubts. Śāṇḍilya Ṛṣi had previously acted as the priest for Nanda Mahārāja and the cowherd men. When Śāṇḍilya Ṛṣi received the message from Parīkṣit Mahārāja, he left his *āśrama* and came before the kings. Vajranābha welcomed the best of sages with the proper ceremonies and had sit him on an elevated seat. Parīkṣit Mahārāja told Śāṇḍilya Ṛṣi everything that Vajranābha had just said. The sage affectionately comforted them with the following words.

Śāṇḍilya Ṛṣi said: Dear Parīkṣit and Vajranābha! I will tell you the secret of Vrajabhūmi. Listen carefully. The meaning of the word "Vraja" is all-pervasive. According to ancient opinions, this land is named Vraja because it is all-pervasive. This land is an all-pervasive spiritual manifestation, situated beyond the three modes of material nature. Therefore this is called Vraja. This land is ever-blissful, effulgent, indestructible, and the abode of liberated souls. Dear kings, in this land of Vraja the self-realized souls and devotees, who relish love of God, constantly experience Kṛṣṇa, whose form is *sac-cid-ānanda*. Śrīmatī Rādhikā, the daughter of Mahārāja Vṛṣabhanu, is like the *ātmā* of Lord Śrī Kṛṣṇa, the son of Nanda Mahārāja. She eternally enjoys pastimes with Kṛṣṇa, and therefore the devotees expert in enjoying transcendental mellows call Kṛṣṇa *ātmārāma*. The meaning of the word *kāma* is desire. In Vraja, Kṛṣṇa's only desire is to engage in pastimes with the cows, and the cowherd boys and girls. Because He always achieves the fulfillment of this desire, He is called *āptakāma*. These pastimes of the Lord are beyond material nature. Whenever the Lord enjoys His pastimes in this world, even ordinary people are benefitted. The creation, maintenance, and annihilation of the material world are carried out respectively by the qualities of passion, goodness, and ignorance. In this way, two types of pastimes of Govinda—transcendental and ordinary—are manifested. His transcendental pastimes are self-evident. This means that these pastimes are relished in Vraja by Śrī Kṛṣṇa, the topmost expert in loving exchanges. The ordinary pastimes consist of delivering the fallen souls and minimizing the burden of the earth in Vraja, Mathurā, and Dvārakā. There cannot be ordinary pastimes without transcendental pastimes. Ordinary pastimes have no entrance into the transcendental pastimes. The pastimes experienced by the two of you are ordinary pastimes. The jurisdiction of the ordinary pastimes stretches from this planet up to the heavenly planets, and Mathurā-maṇḍala is situated within this planet. The famous Vrajabhūmi is situated in this area, and the Lord's confidential pastimes are enacted here. Sometimes these pastimes are manifest to the devotees whose hearts are filled with devotion. At the end of the Dvāpara-yuga in the twenty-eighth yuga cycle, when the Lord's associates who are qualified in the conjugal relationship assemble together, the Lord and His intimate associates descend, just as He recently enacted here. In this way the Lord incarnates whe He desires to relish His pastimes with His intimate associates. At that time all the demigods and other devotees also incarnate with the Lord.

In these pastimes there were three kinds of devotees present. There is no doubt about it. Of these three kinds of devotees, the first are the Lord's intimate eternal associates, the second are those aspiring to become eternal associates, and the third are the demigods and their expansions whom the Lord has previously already sent to Dvārakā.

Now the demigods who had appeared as Yādavas have been sent by the Lord back to their duties in the heavenly planets through the *brāhmaṇa's* curse in the Lord's *mausala-līlā*. And the Lord awarded spiritual forms to the devotees who aspired to become His eternal associates. The Lord then brought these devotees together with His intimate eternal associates of the *vāstavī*, spiritual pastimes and they thus disappeared from the vision of the ordinary people.

Therefore, common people, who are situated in the *vyavaharika* pastimes, are unqualified to enter the Lord's eternal pastimes and see the eternal associates of the *vāstavī* pastimes. That is why this place appears to be devoid of people.

Therefore Vajranābha, you should not worry in the least. By following my instructions and establishing many towns here, you will fulfill all your desires. Wherever Lord Kṛṣṇa has performed His pastimes you should establish towns named after the particular pastime that was performed at that place. In this way you can render very nice service to the transcendental land of Vraja.

Establish your domain at Govardhana, Dirghapura (Deeg), Mathurā, Mahāvana, Nandagrāma (Nandagaon), and Bṛhatsanu (Varṣāṇā). Reside in these pastime sites of Lord Kṛṣṇa and engage in the service of the rivers, mountains, *kuṇḍas*, lakes, and *kuñjas* of Vraja, for by doing so you will be happy and the citizens of your kingdom will prosper. This eternal, cognizant, blissful land of Vraja should be served by you by all efforts. By my blessings you will properly identify all of the places of Lord Kṛṣṇa's pastimes. O Vajranābha, by continually serving Vraja in this way, one day you will meet Śrī Uddhava. Then he will instruct you and your mothers in the mysteries of Vraja and the pastimes of the Lord."

After instructing Vajranābha and Parīkṣit in this way, Śāṇḍilya, the best of the ṛṣis, returned to his *āśrama* while remembering Lord Kṛṣṇa. Parīkṣit and Vajranābha felt great ecstasy after hearing his instructions.

Chapter Two

Parīkṣit and Kṛṣṇa's Wives, While Chanting the Glories of the Lord, met Uddhava

The sages said: O Sūta Gosvāmī, please tell us what Mahārāja Parīkṣit and King Vajranābha did after the best of the *munis*, Śāṇḍilya, returned to his *āśrama*.

Śrīla Sūta Gosvāmī said: Mahārāja Parīkṣit brought thousands of prominent *brāhmaṇas* and *kṣatriyas* from Indraprastha and repopulated Mathurā.

Mahārāja Parīkṣit gave respect to the *brāhmaṇas* and monkeys who were already residing there because he understood they are dear to the Lord. With the help of Mahārāja Parīkṣit and by the mercy of Śāṇḍilya Ṛṣi, Vajranābha gradually searched out the sites where Kṛṣṇa had enjoyed pastimes with His beloved cowherd boyfriends and girlfriends. After properly ascertaining the pastime site, he named the site according to the pastime that was performed there. He thus established and named various towns, *kuṇḍas*, wells, *kuñjas*, and gardens, and he established many Śiva temples. He established Deities of the Lord such as Govindadeva and Harideva, and his entire kingdom became blissful because devotion to Lord Kṛṣṇa was preached everywhere. The citizens always engaged in glorifying Lord Kṛṣṇa and thus merged in an ocean of bliss, they praised the rule of King Vajranābha.

One day, Lord Kṛṣṇa's sixteen thousand queens, who were suffering due to separation, inquired without envy from their fellow wife, Kālindī, who they saw was happy.

Kṛṣṇa's Queens said: O beautiful Kālindī! Just as we are all Kṛṣṇa's wives, so are you. We are all continually burning in the fire of separation and our hearts are distressed with unhappiness due to His absence. But you are not in this condition, you are happy. Why is this? Please tell us the reason.

After understanding the pain of separation felt by her co-wives, Kālindī, with great compassion, smiled and spoke as follows:

Kālindī said: Śrī Rādhikā is the soul of Kṛṣṇa, who is known as *ātmārāma*. I am always engaged in Her service. Due to the influence of this service, the pain of separation could not touch me. All of Kṛṣṇa's consorts are expansions of Śrī Rādhikā. And because Kṛṣṇa is always engaged in enjoying with Śrī Rādhikā, all of Kṛṣṇa's other consorts are automatically being enjoyed by Him. Kṛṣṇa is nondifferent from Śrī Rādhikā, and Śrī Rādhikā is nondifferent from Kṛṣṇa. Their love is manifest in the form of Kṛṣṇa's flute. Śrī Candrāvalī Sakhi is a manifestation of the moonlike nails of Śrī Kṛṣṇacandra. Due to an excessive greed to serve Rādhā-Kṛṣṇa, Candrāvalī has not accepted any other form. But I have seen Śrī Rukmiṇī and other *sakhis* situated in Śrī Rādhikā. And you also have never been separated from Kṛṣṇa, but you are overwhelmed because this mystery is unknown to you. Previously, when Akrūra came to Vṛndāvana, the *gopīs* experienced similar feelings of separation, although actually that was not separation, it was simply a reflection of separation. But when Uddhava came and consoled them, their pain of separation was destroyed. Now if you are able to get the association of Uddhava, then you will also achieve the happiness of eternal pastimes with your beloved Śrī Kṛṣṇa.

Śrīla Sūta Gosvāmī said: O sages! When Kṛṣṇa's queens were instructed in this way, they again addressed the ever-blissful Kālindī. At that time they all hankered for some way to meet Uddhava, so that they could all achieve the great fortune of eternal association with their beloved.

Kṛṣṇa's Queens said: O Sakhi, your life is glorious, because you have never experienced the distress of separation from the Lord of your life. We would also like to become

Rādhā's maidservants, just like you. But, O Kālindī. you have told us that all our desires would be fulfilled by meeting Uddhava, so please tell us how we can meet him.

Śrīla Sūta Gosvāmī said: After hearing the words of her co-wives, Kālindī remembered Kṛṣṇa, who possesses sixty-four qualities in full. Just before Lord Kṛṣṇa returned to His supreme abode, He told His minister Uddhava that Badarikāśrama is a suitable place to engage in spiritual activities. Following that instruction, Uddhava stays there and instructs those who visit him in the same knowledge that was taught to him by the Lord. The Lord taught Uddhava about the mysteries of Vraja, where the fruits of spiritual practice are obtained. But since the personification of the fruits of spiritual practice, Lord Kṛṣṇa, has apparently left this place, Uddhava is also no longer seen here. Being desirous to associate with the dust of Vraja, however, Uddhava is certainly residing near Govardhana at Sakhīsthalī in the form of a creeper. Uddhava is the personification of Lord Kṛṣṇa's festivals. Therefore go to Kusuma-sarovara with Vajranābha and organize a festival there. Assemble the Lord's devotees and start a big festival by chanting the Lord's holy names and pastimes accompanied by *vīṇās*, flutes, and *mṛdaṅgas*.

In this way when the festival expands, Uddhava will certainly appear there. And by his mercy all your desires will be fulfilled.

Śrīla Sūta Gosvāmī said: After hearing Kālindī speak these words Lord Kṛṣṇa's queens were greatly pleased. After they offered their respects to Kālindī they went and told Vajranābha and Parīkṣit everything that they had heard.

After hearing their narration, Mahārāja Parīkṣit was greatly pleased and accompanied them to Kusuma-sarovara and began organizing a festival there. They began a festival of *nama saṅkīrtana* at Sakhīsthalī, a short distance from Govardhana. As they glorified Lord Kṛṣṇa at that place where He always enjoys pastimes with His beloved, the daughter of Vṛṣabhanu, the place was transformed into an extraordinary scene. They became fully absorbed in glorifying Lord Kṛṣṇa.

At that time, from amidst the grass, vines, and creepers Śrī Uddhava appeared before everyone. His complexion was bluish, and he wore yellow garments. He was decorated with a garland of forest flowers and guñjā, and he repeatedly glorified Kṛṣṇa, the lover of the *gopīs*. Then the beauty of the *saṅkīrtana* festival increased many times over just as when the moonshine falls on a crystal house. Similarly everyone was merged in an ocean of bliss by his appearance there, and they forgot what they were doing. When they regained their external consciousness, they saw Uddhava, who resembles Lord Kṛṣṇa, and by worshiping him, they fulfilled all their desires.

Chapter Three

The Glories of *Śrīmad-Bhāgavatam*, the Speaker and the Hearer's Attainment of the Supreme Abode

Śrīla Sūta Gosvāmī said: Seeing everyone engaged in glorifying Lord Kṛṣṇa, Śrī Uddhava offered his respects and embraced them. He spoke with Mahārāja Parīkṣit.

Śrī Uddhava said: O King, you are certainly glorious. Your desire has been fulfilled by your undivided devotional service to Lord Kṛṣṇa, because your mind is absorbed in this *saṅkīrtana* festival. It is your great fortune that you have such incomparable affection for Vajranābha and Kṛṣṇa's queens. This is quite proper because Lord Kṛṣṇa has given you this body and power. Among the residents of Dvārakā, they are the most glorious. There is no doubt about it. Lord Kṛṣṇa ordered Arjuna to escort them to Vraja so that they could reside there. Illuminated by the effulgence of Śrīmatī Rādhārāṇī's face, the moonlike mind of Lord Kṛṣṇa constantly illuminates Śrī Vṛndāvana, the site of Rādhā's pastimes. Śrī Kṛṣṇacandra is eternally complete. Thousands of spiritual sparks oscillate in all directions from His sixty-four qualities. The full moonlike Kṛṣṇa, who possesses sixty-four prominent qualities, is constantly illuminating this land of Vraja. O King, the right foot of Lord Kṛṣṇa is the residence of Vajranābha, who destroys the fear of his subordinates. In this incarnation, Lord Śrī Kṛṣṇa has bewildered everyone through Yogamāyā.

By her influence, they have forgotten their constitutional position and they appear miserable. There is no doubt about it. Without Kṛṣṇa manifesting in one's heart, no one can realise his constitutional position. Kṛṣṇa's manifestation within the hearts of the living entities has been covered by Māyā. When Lord Hari personally appears at the end of Dvāpara-yuga in the twenty-eighth yuga cycle and lifts the covering of Māyā, then He becomes manifest. O Mahārāja Parīkṣit, the time of those manifest pastimes has recently ended. Therefore I will now tell you the means of having Kṛṣṇa manifest within one's heart. When Lord Kṛṣṇa is unmanifest, He will appear from *Śrīmad-Bhāgavatam*. Whenever and wherever the devotee Bhāgavata hears and recites the book Bhāgavata, at that time and at that place Lord Kṛṣṇa personally appears. Wherever a verse of *Śrīmad-Bhāgavatam*, or even a half-verse of *Śrīmad-Bhāgavatam*, is recited, Lord Kṛṣṇa and His beloved *gopīs* manifest there. After attaining a human birth in the land of Bharata, those who do not hear *Śrīmad-Bhāgavatam* due to sinful activities are committing suicide. A person who regularly hears or recites *Śrīmad-Bhāgavatam* delivers the forefathers of his wife, mother, and father.

By studying and hearing *Śrīmad-Bhāgavatam*, *brāhmaṇas* are enlightened with knowledge, *kṣatriyas* achieve victory over their enemies, *vaiśyas* acquire wealth, and *śūdras* are freed from disease. Women and lower class people all achieve the fulfillment of their desires. Therefore what fortunate person will not regularly hear and chant the *Śrīmad-Bhāgavatam*?

After many lifetimes of performing pious activities, when a person achieves full perfection then he obtains the *Śrīmad-Bhāgavatam*. By reading *Śrīmad-Bhāgavatam* one's devotional sentiments are awakened and Lord Kṛṣṇa manifests within the heart.

Long ago, Bṛhaspati, the spiritual master of the demigods, heard the *Śrīmad-Bhāgavatam* by the mercy of Sāṅkhyāyana Ṛṣi, and Bṛhaspati has narrated the same to me. I was therefore able to become the dear friend of Lord Kṛṣṇa. O Mahārāja Parīkṣit, Bṛhaspati has told me one story. Please hear it from me. From this story one can know the method of hearing *Śrīmad-Bhāgavatam* from the proper authorities.

Bṛhaspati said: O Uddhava, when Lord Kṛṣṇa accepted the *puruṣa* incarnations and glanced over material nature to create, then the three personalities—Brahmā, Viṣṇu, and Śiva—appeared along with the three modes of material nature—*sattva*, *raja*, and *tama*. Lord Kṛṣṇa then assigned the work of creation, maintenance, and destruction to the three predominating deities. Lord Brahmā appeared from the lotus sprouted from the navel of the Lord.

Lord Brahmā said: O Lord! I offer my respectful obeisances unto You. Because You lie in the transcendental water known as *nāra*, You are known as Nārāyaṇa. And as the original cause of everything You are *ādi-puruṣa*, the original person. O Lord, although I am sinful and full of the mode of passion, You have engaged me in the work of creation. But I pray for Your blessing that my engagement in the activities of creation will not be an impediment in my remembering Your lotus feet.

Bṛhaspati said: After Brahmā offered these prayers to Lord Nārāyaṇa, at that time, long ago, the Lord gave Brahmā the *Śrīmad-Bhāgavatam* and told him: "To achieve fulfillment of your desires, always serve this *Śrīmad-Bhāgavatam.*" On receiving *Śrīmad-Bhāgavatam*, Lord Brahmā was greatly pleased. In order to attain Lord Kṛṣṇa and penetrate the seven coverings, he recited *Śrīmad-Bhāgavatam* for seven days. All Brahmā's desires were fulfilled by serving *Śrīmad-Bhāgavatam* for that seven day sacrifice. Since then he has always been engaged in expanding the creation and repeatedly reciting the *Śrīmad-Bhāgavatam*. As done by Brahmā, Lord Viṣṇu also prayed for the fulfillment of His desires so that He could engage in maintaining the creation.

Lord Viṣṇu said: O Lord, I will accept the paths of *pravṛtti* and *nirvṛtti* due to the need for fruitive activities and philosophical knowledge. Following Your order, I will duly maintain the living entities. In due course of time, whenever there is a decline in religious principles, I will accept various incarnations in order to reestablish the principles of religion. I will certainly award the fruits of their sacrifice to those who desire material enjoyment, and I will award five kinds of liberation, beginning with *sālokya*, to those who are renounced and desirous to achieve liberation. But please tell Me how to maintain My dear Lakṣmī and those who have no desire for the five kinds of liberation.

After hearing Viṣṇu's prayers, the primeval Lord, Nārāyaṇa, told Him: "In order to achieve the fulfillment of all Your desires, just recite *Śrīmad-Bhāgavatam*." Lord Viṣṇu was very pleased to receive this instruction from Lord Nārāyaṇa. He engaged every month along with Lakṣmīdevī in the recitation of *Śrīmad-Bhāgavatam*. Thus He was able to maintain the creation. Whenever Lord Viṣṇu recites *Śrīmad-Bhāgavatam*, Lakṣmīdevī listens. This takes one full month. And whenever Lakṣmīdevī speaks *Śrīmad-Bhāgavatam* and Viṣṇu listens, it takes two months to relish the mellows of the *Śrīmad-Bhāgavatam*. At that time the taste of those topics become extremely palatable. The reason for this is that Viṣṇu is engaged in maintaining the creation, therefore He is preoccupied with many thoughts. But this is not the case with Lakṣmīdevī, who is fully peaceful. The topics of *Śrīmad-Bhāgavatam* are therefore more elaborately manifested in her heart.

Thereafter the Lord engaged Śiva in the work of annihilation. In order to expand his own ability, Śiva also prayed to the Lord.

Śrī Rudra said: O Lord of lords, I have the power to engage in three types of destruction—perpetual, occasional, and partial. But, O Lord, I have no power at all for the final destruction. For this reason I am very unhappy. I am therefore praying to You.

Bṛhaspati said: Hearing the prayers of Rudra, Lord Nārāyaṇa also instructed him on the topics of *Śrīmad-Bhāgavatam*. Śrī Rudradeva then conquered the mode of ignorance just by serving *Śrīmad-Bhāgavatam*. Sadāśiva Rudra then recited *Śrīmad-Bhāgavatam* over a period of one year. He thus attained the power of final destruction.

Śrī Uddhava said: I have heard these glories of *Śrīmad-Bhāgavatam* from the mouth of Śrī Bṛhaspati, my spiritual master. Now I offer my respectful obeisances to him for I have become happy by hearing the instructions of *Śrīmad-Bhāgavatam*. According to the Vaiṣṇava tradition, I served *Śrīmad-Bhāgavatam* for just one month. Due to the influence of this service, I have become the dear friend of Lord Kṛṣṇa, and He therefore sent me to Vṛndāvana to serve his beloved *gopīs*. Although Kṛṣṇa eternally enjoys pastimes in Vṛndāvana, His beloved *gopīs* were afflicted by feelings of separation. He therefore sent me here to impart the teachings of *Śrīmad-Bhāgavatam* to the *gopīs*. The *gopīs* of Vraja were thus freed from the pains of separation by accepting the teachings of *Śrīmad-Bhāgavatam* according to their own intelligence. Even though I do not understand the mystery of *Śrīmad-Bhāgavatam*, still I have experienced the wonder of this great literature. When the demigods, headed by Lord Brahmā, prayed to Lord Kṛṣṇa that He shall return to His own abode, at that time, under a banyan tree, the Lord personally taught me the mystery of *Śrīmad-Bhāgavatam*. As a result of that instruction my intelligence became fixed and I proceeded to Badarikāśrama and attained perfection. Since then I am living here in Vraja as a creeper.

O Parīkṣit, I am therefore living here at Nārada-kuṇḍa. The devotees will realise Lord Kṛṣṇa by serving *Śrīmad-Bhāgavatam*. Therefore I will explain *Śrīmad-Bhāgavatam* for the benefit of the devotees of the Lord. This will be possible only with your help.

Śrīla Sūta Gosvāmī said: After hearing this, Mahārāja Parīkṣit offered his obeisances to Uddhava and said to him: O Uddhava, servant of Lord Hari! You should certainly narrate *Śrīmad-Bhāgavatam*. Whatever is necessary for me to do in this regard, please order me.

Uddhava was most pleased on hearing Parīkṣit Mahārāja speak in this way and said: O King! Since Lord Kṛṣṇa has left this world, the influence of Kali-yuga has become very prominent. Whenever auspicious activities are being performed Kali certainly creates disturbances. Therefore you should go out and subdue the influence of Kali everywhere. I will remain here by your arrangement and recite *Śrīmad-Bhāgavatam* for one month according to Vaiṣṇava tradition. The audience will thus relish the mellows of *Śrīmad-Bhāgavatam* and attain the Lord's eternal abode.

Hearing Śrī Uddhava's instructions, Mahārāja Parīkṣit was pleased by the thought of subduing Kali, but somewhat in anxiety he disclosed his mind to Uddhava.

Mahārāja Parīkṣit said: O Prabhu! I am eager to bring Kali-yuga under my control as you have instructed, but then how will I hear the *Śrīmad-Bhāgavatam*? I have also come to take shelter at your feet, so you should also be merciful to me.

Hearing the king's words, Uddhava said: O King, there is no need for you to be worried, for you are the most eligible candidate to receive the *Śrīmad-Bhāgavatam*. People in this world are always engaged in various kinds of fruitive activities and they do not even know the importance of hearing *Śrīmad-Bhāgavatam*. O King, by your mercy many people in this land of Bharata-varsa will achieve eternal happiness by hearing *Śrīmad-Bhāgavatam*. The great sage Śrīla Śukadeva Gosvāmī, who is the representative of Lord Kṛṣṇa, the son of Nanda Mahārāja, will recite *Śrīmad-Bhāgavatam* to you. There is no doubt about it. O King, you will attain the eternal abode of Lord Kṛṣṇa, the king of Vraja, by hearing *Śrīmad-Bhāgavatam*, and *Śrīmad-Bhāgavatam* will then later be propagated throughout the world.

Therefore, O King, prepare yourself to subdue Kali.

After Uddhava spoke in this way, Mahārāja Parīkṣit offered obeisances to Uddhava and circumambulated him, and he then left to eradicate Kali's influence in all directions.

Vajranābha then installed his son, Pratibāhu, as the king of Mathurā. He stayed with his grandmothers simply for the purpose of hearing *Śrīmad-Bhāgavatam*. Then at that place near Govardhana, Śrī Uddhava recited *Śrīmad-Bhāgavatam* for one month. While relishing the topics of *Śrīmad-Bhāgavatam* the listeners saw Kṛṣṇa manifest everywhere along with His transcendental pastimes. The listeners could see themselves taking part in those transcendental pastimes. Vajranābha saw himself situated at the right lotus foot of Lord Kṛṣṇa, and thus felt relief from the pains of separation and pleased with the beauty of that scene. All his grandmothers, headed by Rohiṇī, were most surprised to see themselves situated as the effulgence and portion of the moonlike Kṛṣṇa, who inaugurates the night of the rasa dance. Being cured of the disease of separation from their beloved life and soul, they entered their supreme destination.

Other people who were present there also disappeared and entered the Lord's eternal pastimes. They all enjoy pastimes with Kṛṣṇa in the *kuñjas* of Govardhana, the pasturing grounds and forest of Vṛndāvana. The devotees who are greedy for attaining the mellows of transcendental love can always see these pastimes.

Śrīla Sūta Gosvāmī said: Whoever chants or hears these pastimes of attaining the Lord's lotus feet will certainly attain those lotus feet, and all his miseries from time immemorial will be destroyed forever.

Chapter Four

The Characteristics of *Śrīmad-Bhāgavatam*, the Symptoms of the Speaker and the Listener, and Establishing the Procedure for Hearing

The sages headed by Śaunaka said: O Sūta, may you live a long life and continue instructing us. Today we have heard the wonderful glories of *Śrīmad-Bhāgavatam* from your mouth. O Sūta, now please mercifully describe for us the characteristics of *Śrīmad-Bhāgavatam*, its authenticity, the procedure for hearing, and the symptoms of the speaker and the listener.

Śrīla Sūta Gosvāmī said: The characteristics of *Śrīmad-Bhāgavatam* and the Personality of Godhead are both eternal, full of knowledge and bliss.

You should know that whatever transcendental, sweet words come from the mouths of those whose hearts are attached to Kṛṣṇa, those statements are *Śrīmad-Bhāgavatam*. You should also know that *Śrīmad-Bhāgavatam* consists of knowledge, realized knowledge, and the four limbs of devotional service, such as hearing and chanting. It is expert in eradicating the influence of māyā, the illusory energy.

Who can understand the authenticity of *Śrīmad-Bhāgavatam*, which is the unlimited sound representation of the Lord? In the beginning of creation, Lord Hari spoke four verses to Lord Brahmā. O *brāhmaṇas*, only personalities such as Brahmā, Viṣṇu, and Śiva are able to attain their desired goal by merging into the ocean of the unlimited *Śrīmad-Bhāgavatam*, others are not able.

Whatever Śrīla Vedavyāsa has described in the conversation between Parīkṣit Mahārāja and Śukadeva Gosvāmī for the benefit of the less intelligent, that is known as *Śrīmad-Bhāgavatam*. *Śrīmad-Bhāgavatam* consists of 18,000 verses, and it is the only shelter for those who are captured by the crocodile of Kali.

Now I will describe those who listen to *Śrīmad-Bhāgavatam*. There are two types of listeners—superior and inferior. The superior listeners are of four kinds—namely, *cātaka* bird, swan, parrot, and fish. And the inferior listeners are also of four kinds—wolf, *bhurunda* bird, bull, and camel.

Just as the *cātaka* bird does not take water from any source other than the raincloud, one who does not hear any scripture or book other than those related with Lord Kṛṣṇa is called a *cātaka* listener.

Just as the swan can extract milk from a mixture of milk and water, one who can extract the essential topics of Lord Kṛṣṇa while listening to various topics is called a swan listener.

Just as a parrot can recite to its master and others whatever it is taught, one who can nicely repeat the topics he has heard from the scriptures to his *guru* and other listeners is called a parrot listener.

Just as the fish that is situated in an ocean of condensed milk quietly drinks milk without blinking its eyes, one who quietly hears *Śrīmad-Bhāgavatam* while relishing the topics and staring unblinking at the speaker is called a fish listener.

Just as the cry of the wolf frightens the deer which is attracted by the sweet sound of a flute in the forest, the foolish listener whose loud noises create pain to the devotees engaged in hearing the sweet topics of *Śrīmad-Bhāgavatam* is called a wolf listener.

Just as the *bhurunda* bird that lives in the Himalayas tells others whatever instruction it has heard without practicing himself, one who teaches others but does not follow those instructions is called a *bhurunda* listener.

Just as the bull does not distinguish between eating sweet grapes or pungent oilcakes, the blind person who listens to everything but has no intelligence to discriminate between good and bad is called a bull listener.

Just as the camel rejects the sweet mango leaves and chews instead the bitter nimb leaves, one who rejects the sweet narrations about the Lord and hears instead mundane topics is called a camel listener.

Apart from these two categories of listeners, there are many further subclassifications such as bumblebees and asses which one should understand by the symptoms of their normal behavior.

Speakers say the topmost listener is he who comes before the speaker, offers due obeisances, and is eager and expert in hearing the pastimes of Lord Hari, after rejecting all types of mundane topics. He humbly engages in hearing with folded hands like a disciple, he has full faith in the Lord, he is attached to asking questions, and he always contemplates the subject he has heard. He is a dear friend of the Lord's devotees.

The topmost speakers, who are respected by all sages, are those whose hearts are attached to the Lord without hankering for anything else. They are the well-wishers of all, they are merciful to the fallen, and they are expert in learning the truth by various arguments.

Now, O *brāhmaṇas*, please hear the procedure for hearing *Śrīmad-Bhāgavatam* in the land of Bharata. Simply by hearing these rules one enjoys everlasting happiness.

There are four kinds of service to the *Śrīmad-Bhāgavatam—sattvic*, *rajasic*, *tamasic*, and *nirguṇa*.

Enthusiastic service which is joyfully performed in seven days, like a pompous sacrifice with various types of worshipable ingredients and hard labor, is called *rajasic bhāgavata-sevā*

Service which is peacefully performed over a month or two, while relishing the topics and thus increasing one's ecstasy, is called *sattvic bhāgavata-sevā*.

Service which continues for one year, which is performed lazily yet faithfully, which gives happiness, and in which both rememberance and forgetfulness are present, is called *tamasic bhāgavata-sevā*.

Service in which there is no consideration of time factor but continues on with love and devotion, is called *nirguṇa bhāgavata-sevā*.

Please know for certain that Mahārāja Parīkṣit and Śukadeva Gosvāmī performed *nirguṇa bhagavata-sevā*. Although the hearing continued for only seven days, that was because Mahārāja Parīkṣit's life continued for that duration only.

One should hear *Śrīmad-Bhāgavatam* in any place or in any way one desires—whether *sattvic*, *rajasic*, *tamasic*, or *nirguṇa*.

Śrīmad-Bhāgavatam is the only wealth of those who are completely devoid of material desires, and greedy to relish hearing and chanting the pastimes of Lord Kṛṣṇa.

Śrīmad-Bhāgavatam is the medicine to cure the material disease of those who are indifferent to the miseries of material existence and desire liberation. Therefore everyone should carefully serve *Śrīmad-Bhāgavatam*.

The *karmīs*, who are greedy for material enjoyment and advancement in material life, will attain everything they desire just by serving *Śrīmad-Bhāgavatam* in Kali-yuga.

In Kali-yuga it is extremely rare to attain perfection on the path of *karma* due to a lack of physical ability, wealth, and knowledge. Therefore those who wish auspiciousness should serve *Śrīmad-Bhāgavatam* in all respects.

The topics of *Śrīmad-Bhāgavatam* are able to give one wealth, children, wife, elephants, horses, fame, palatial residences, and a kingdom without rivals.

By serving the *Śrīmad-Bhāgavatam* one with material desires can enjoy all his desired results in this world and attain the abode of the Supreme Lord after giving up his body.

One should serve anyone absorbed in discussing the topics of *Śrīmad-Bhāgavatam* with one's body and wealth.

By serving those who are absorbed in *Śrīmad-Bhāgavatam*, one can attain the results of serving *Śrīmad-Bhāgavatam*.

There are two types of reciters and listeners of the *Śrīmad-Bhāgavatam*. Some desire Kṛṣṇa and some desire material prosperity. Material prosperity refers to anything not related to Kṛṣṇa. So if the reciter and listener are of the same category, then the happiness from serving *Śrīmad-Bhāgavatam* increases.

If the reciter and the listener are not of the same category, then there is a contradiction and no result is attained. Such a situation is called *rasābhāsa*, or overlapping of mellows. But a person who desires Kṛṣṇa—whether as a speaker or listener—will certainly attain his goal, even if delayed.

The speaker and listener who desire wealth will attain their desired goal if they act under rules and regulations. But those transcendental speakers and listeners who desire Kṛṣṇa will undoubtedly attain their goal even if they do not follow the rules and regulations, because love of God is the only rule for such persons.

A person with material desires must rigidly follow all the rules through to completion. He should regularly take bath in the morning, and after performing his daily worship he should accept the *caraṇāmṛtā* of Lord Hari.

Thereafter the speaker or listener should worship their spiritual master and *Śrīmad-Bhāgavatam* with proper ingredients. They should hear and chant *Śrīmad-Bhāgavatam* in a joyful mood.

One should take a vow of silence, and eat only milk or sweet rice. He should sleep on the ground, give up all anger and greed, and practice the vow of *brahmācārya*.

After finishing the recitation of *Śrīmad-Bhāgavatam*, one should constantly chant the holy name of the Lord, and on the last day he should remain awake at night and then feed the *brāhmaṇas* and satisfy them with charity.

One should then worship his spiritual master after offering him cloth, ornaments, and cows. Anyone who renders service to the *Śrīmad-Bhāgavatam* according to these regulations will surely achieve the fulfillment of all his desires.

A person with material desires can obtain a beautiful wife, children, kingdom, or wealth if he so desires. But such desires are a mockery to the stature of *Śrīmad-Bhāgavatam*.

Śrīmad-Bhāgavatam is the ripened fruit of the desire tree of Vedic literature. It has been bestowed to the world in this age of Kali by Śrī Śukadeva Gosvāmī and has become more nectarean by the touch of his lips. It is the direct means of attaining Lord Kṛṣṇa, and it eternally bestows love of God.

Chapter Five

Description of the Results of Hearing *Śrīmad-Bhāgavatam*, and the Condition of Those who are Averse to such Hearing

The Supreme Lord said: O Grandfather Brahmā, one should regularly hear the famous *Śrīmad-Bhāgavatam* with faith. Know for certain that such hearing is the only means of satisfying Me.

One who daily reads *Śrīmad-Bhāgavatam* will attain with every syllable the results of giving a brown cow in charity.

One who daily reads or hears even a half or a quarter of a verse of *Śrīmad-Bhāgavatam* attains the results of giving one thousand cows in charity.

My dear son, one who daily reads *Śrīmad-Bhāgavatam* with full concentration attains the results of studying the eighteen *Purāṇas*.

Vaiṣṇavas like Prahlāda Mahārāja are always present wherever the topics of *Śrīmad-Bhāgavatam* are discussed. Those who worship *Śrīmad-Bhāgavatam* are beyond the jurisdiction of Kali.

Those persons who worship the Vaiṣṇava literature *Śrīmad-Bhāgavatam* in their house are freed from all sins and they become worshipable by even the demigods.

In the age of Kali, I become very pleased with those who regularly worship *Śrīmad-Bhāgavatam* in their house and dance without fear.

O My dear son, as long as *Śrīmad-Bhāgavatam* is present in one's house, for that long his forefathers consume milk, ghee, honey, and water.

One who with devotion gives the gift of *Śrīmad-Bhāgavatam* to a Vaiṣṇava resides in My abode for millions of *kalpas*.

One who always worships *Śrīmad-Bhāgavatam* in his house satisfies the demigods for the duration of one *kalpa*.

If even a half or a quarter of a verse of *Śrīmad-Bhāgavatam* is kept in one's house that is glorious. For what is the need of accumulating thousands of other literatures?

In Kali-yuga, one who does not keep *Śrīmad-Bhāgavatam* in his house can never be delivered from the control of Yamarāja.

In Kali-yuga, how can one be considered a Vaiṣṇava who does not keep *Śrīmad-Bhāgavatam* in his house? He is more abominable than a *caṇḍāla*.

My dear son, lord of the universe. For My pleasure and the pleasure of the Vaiṣṇavas one should keep *Śrīmad-Bhāgavatam* with devotion.

In Kali-yuga, wherever the auspicious *Śrīmad-Bhāgavatam* is recited, I reside, along with all the demigods.

My dear son, all the holy rivers, *kuṇḍas*, and lakes, all sacrifices, the seven sacred cities— Ayodhyā, Mathurā, Māyā (Haridvāra), Kāśī, Kāñci, Avantī (Ujjain), and Dvārakā—and all the holy mountains are present where *Śrīmad-Bhāgavatam* is discussed.

O lord of the universe, one should hear *Śrīmad-Bhāgavatam* in order to attain fame, religiosity, victory, freedom from sin, or liberation.

By hearing *Śrīmad-Bhāgavatam* one becomes religious and he lives a long life, free from disease and all sinful reactions.

O lord of the universe, I speak the truth: those who do not hear the topmost literature, *Śrīmad-Bhāgavatam*, or do not express happiness after hearing it are kept under Yamarāja's jurisdiction.

O My dear son, there is no one more sinful than one who does not go anywhere to hear *Śrīmad-Bhāgavatam*, especially on the day of Ekādaśī.

I reside in the house of one who has kept there a verse, a half verse, or even a quarter of a verse of *Śrīmad-Bhāgavatam*.

The purity one attains by hearing *Śrīmad-Bhāgavatam* cannot be attained by visiting Badarikāśrama or taking bath in the confluence at Prayāga.

O four-headed Brahmā, I go wherever the topics of *Śrīmad-Bhāgavatam* are discussed, just as a cow spontaneously follows her calf.

I never leave one who enjoys speaking or hearing *Śrīmad-Bhāgavatam*. One who does not offer respects after seeing the auspicious *Śrīmad-Bhāgavatam* loses the pious credits he accumulated over the past year.

I am unlimitedly pleased with one who stands in respect and then offers obeisances upon seeing *Śrīmad-Bhāgavatam*.

A person who circumambulates *Śrīmad-Bhāgavatam* achieves the results of an *aśvamedha-yajña* with every step. Of this there is no doubt.

For one who stands in respect and then offers obeisances upon seeing *Śrīmad-Bhāgavatam*, I offer him wealth, wife, children, and devotional service.

My dear son, I am controlled by those who worship *Śrīmad-Bhāgavatam* with sixteen ingredients and hear *Śrīmad-Bhāgavatam* with devotion.

O Brahmā, O Suvrata, among all types of festivals, the festival of discussing *Śrīmad-Bhāgavatam* is the topmost. Those who participate in such festivals for My pleasure and hear *Śrīmad-Bhāgavatam* with devotion and those who worship *Śrīmad-Bhāgavatam* with cloth, ornaments, flowers, lamp, and incense certainly control Me just as a chaste wife controls her good husband.